Contents

Motion

Planning the Unit 2

Curriculum Correlation 4

Addressing Student Preconceptions 5

Opportunities for Ongoing Assessment ... 6

Unit Overview 7

Launch: Motion at the Circus 8

1: Kinds of Motion 10

2: Balloon Rockets in Motion 13

3: Forces and Motion 16

4: Pendulums 20

5: Circles into Lines 24

6: Friction Can Be a Drag! 27

7: Reducing Friction 30

8: Simple Machines 33

9: Levers 36

10: Combining Simple Machines 40

11: Collisions 43

12: Motion and the Environment 46

13: Handbook for Young Inventors 49

End-of-Unit Assessment Opportunities ... 52

Design Project:
Design Your Own Machine! 53

Unit Review

Demonstrate What You Know 55

Explain Your Stuff 56

How Did You Do? 57

Reproducible Line Masters

LM 1 Ongoing Assessment Tracking
Sheet 58

LM 2 End-of-Unit Assessment Summary
Chart 59

LM 3 Design Project Planner: Design Your
Own Machine! 60

LM 4 Design Project Rubric 61

LM 5 Student Achievement Summary .. 62

LM 6 Student Self-Assessment Rubric .. 63

LM 7 Explain Your Stuff 64

LM 8 Unit Test 66

LM 9 How Did You Do? 68

LM 10 The Inquiry Process for Science .. 69

LM 11 The Design Process for
Technology 70

Reproducible Activity Centres

AC 1 Design Challenge: The Ultimate
Balloon Rocket! 71

AC 2 All Fall Down! 72

AC 3 Design Challenge: Make Time ... 73

AC 4 Return of the Balloon Rocket ... 74

AC 5 Design Challenge:
The Tree House 75

AC 6 Out of the Groove 76

Planning the Unit

Activity	Type of Activity	Time	Required Materials	Optional Materials
Launch: Motion at the Circus	Discussion	1 class period	no materials required	
1 Kinds of Motion	Reading	1 class period	no materials required	
2 Balloon Rockets in Motion	Guided Inquiry	1–2 class periods	**for each group** • oblong balloon • 4-m string or nylon line • ruler or measuring tape • drinking straw • chair • desk • tape • cardboard • pencil • scissors	• timing device
3 Forces and Motion	Reading	1–2 class periods	no materials required	
4 Pendulums	Guided Inquiry/ Open Inquiry	1–2 class periods	**for each group** • string • metal washers • pencil • paper clips • scissors • 30-cm ruler • stopwatch or watch with second hand	
5 Circles into Lines	Guided Inquiry	1–2 class periods	**for each group** • shoe box • tape • nails • pen • scissors • ruler • paper • 6 flexible straws	
6 Friction Can Be a Drag!	Guided Inquiry	1–2 class periods	**for each pair** • two identical blocks of wood • piece of cardboard with a hook in the end • flat piece of wood • spring scale • piece of carpet • piece of linoleum	
7 Reducing Friction	Reading	1–2 class periods	no materials required	
8 Simple Machines	Design	1–2 class periods	**for each group** • block of wood with a hook on it • several other blocks of wood • straws • long thin pieces of wood • bamboo skewers • spring scale • wheel and axle • smooth board for a ramp • metre stick • a pile of books (4 or 5) • gears • string • several pulleys • tape • 2 chairs	• saw • drill • hammer • nails
9 Levers	Reading/Guided Inquiry	1–2 class periods	**for each group** • metre stick • fulcrum (wooden block) • 200-g mass • tape • spring scale • set of small masses • supporting wire or string loops • 3 books (to stand the fulcrum on)	
10 Combining Simple Machines	Guided Inquiry	1–2 class periods	**for each pair** • variety of household items such as bicycle, can opener, nut cracker, scissors, wind-up toy car, eggbeater, corkscrew	
11 Collisions	Guided Inquiry	1–2 class periods	**for each pair** • 30-cm plastic ruler with a centre groove or similar object • 7 identical marbles • book	
12 Motion and the Environment	Reading	1–2 class periods	no materials required	
13 Handbook for Young Inventors	Reading	1–2 class periods	no materials required	
Design Project: Design Your Own Machine!	Design	2–3 class periods	**for each group** • paper • pencils • pencil crayons or • various materials for	

Line Masters	Activity Centres	Build On What You Know	Bookshelf
LM 1		• begin collecting photographs or drawings of motion to create a class display	
LM 1		• classify the kinds of motion in the pictures collected • add more pictures to the display, including pictures of machines with moving parts	• Macauley, David, *The Way Things Work* (Houghton Mifflin Co., 1988).
LM 1	AC 1 – Design Challenge		• Morgan, Sally, *Movement* (Facts on File, 1993).
LM 1	AC 2 – For Enrichment	• select 2 pictures from the display and add arrows to show the forces acting on the object that cause it to move	• Lafferty, Peter, *Force and Motion* (Stoddart Publishing Co., 1992).
LM 1 LM 10	AC 3 – Design Challenge		• Bender, Lionel, *Eyewitness Books – Invention* (Stoddart Publishing Co., 1991).
LM 1			• Ardley, Neil, *The Science Book of Machines* (Doubleday Canada Limited, 1992). • Macauley, David, *The Way Things Work* (Houghton Mifflin Co., 1988).
LM 1	AC 4 – For Enrichment		• *The Jumbo Book of Science* (Kids Can Press, 1994).
LM 1		• find 3 pictures from the display in which friction would affect the motion • explain the friction, and suggest how it could be increased or reduced	
LM 1 LM 11			
LM 1	AC 5 – Design Challenge	• add a picture of each type of lever to the display • label the picture to show fulcrum, effort force, load	
LM 1		• add pictures of mechanical devices that include simple machines to the display • write captions for the pictures	
LM 1	AC 6 – For Enrichment	• find pictures of sports collisions to add to the display • write a caption to describe the transfer of kinetic energy in each picture	
LM 1			
LM 1			• Caney, Steven, *Steven Caney's Invention Book* (Workman Publishing, 1985). • Taylor, Barbara, *Be An Inventor* (Harcourt Brace Jovanovich, 1987).
LM 4 LM 3 LM 1		• try to find pictures of Rube Goldberg machines to add to the display • describe the motion involved in each picture	

Curriculum Correlation

Learning Expectations (LE)	Activities													
By the end of Grade 6, students will:	1	2	3	4	5	6	7	8	9	10	11	12	13	DP
Understanding Basic Concepts														
1 describe, using their observations, ways in which mechanical devices and systems produce a linear output from a rotary input	X				X									
2 describe, using their observations, the purposes or uses of three classes of simple levers									X					
3 demonstrate an understanding of how linkages (systems of levers) transmit motion and force									X	X				
4 demonstrate awareness that a moving mass has kinetic energy that can be transferred to a stationary object											X			
5 demonstrate awareness that friction transforms kinetic energy into heat energy							X							
6 investigate ways of reducing friction so that an object can be moved more easily		X				X	X							
Developing Skills of Inquiry, Design, and Communication														
7 design and make mechanical devices that change the direction and speed of an input to produce a desired output and that perform a useful function		X			X									X
8 formulate questions about and identify needs and problems related to structures and mechanisms in the environment, and explore possible answers and solutions												X		X
9 plan investigations for some of these answers and solutions, identifying variables that need to be held constant to ensure a fair test and identifying criteria for assessing solutions				X										X
10 use appropriate vocabulary, including correct science and technology terminology, in describing their investigations and observations	X	X	X	X	X				X		X			
11 compile data gathered through investigation in order to record and present results, using tally charts, tables, labelled graphs, and scatter plots produced by hand or with a computer						X				X				
12 communicate the procedures and results of investigations for specific purposes and to specific audiences, using media works, written notes and descriptions, charts, drawings, and oral presentations	X		X	X		X	X	X	X	X	X		X	
Relating Science and Technology to the World Outside the School														
13 make use of the physical and aesthetic properties of natural and manufactured materials when designing a product													X	
14 show awareness of the effect on a design of the unavailability of specific materials													X	
15 write a plan outlining the different materials and processes involved in producing a product													X	X
16 identify various criteria for selecting a product													X	X
17 describe modifications that could improve the action of a variety of devices at home				X						X			X	
18 show an understanding of the impact of moving mechanisms on the environment and on living things										X		X		
19 compare qualitatively the effort required to move a load a given distance using different devices and systems							X	X						
20 describe how different devices and systems have been used by different cultures to meet similar needs									X	X				

Addressing Student Preconceptions of Motion

Children have two important misconceptions about force and motion: (1) a constant force is needed to maintain constant motion, and (2) friction is not a force. Three hundred years ago, Isaac Newton introduced his famous three laws. These laws established the fact that constant motion is actually natural, and is what takes place when there is no force of friction. Because friction acts almost everywhere, these new ideas initially seemed strange. With the space travel of today, we have more experience with friction-less situations. However, as research reports show, most children and many adults still believe in the pre-scientific notion that an object will stop if no force is exerted on it. (Objects stop moving because the force of friction slows them down. Far out in space, where there is no friction or gravity, objects keep moving with constant velocity in a straight line.)

Launch: Motion at the Circus
The questions in the launch will orient students to the different kinds of motion and provide the opportunity to elicit student views on motion. You might ask them about motion in space: For spacecraft, is a force always needed to maintain motion?

Lesson 1: Kinds of Motion
You might ask students if one of these four types of motion is special. For example, which motion would occur naturally if there were absolutely no friction, and no force such as gravity, no swing seats and cables, no rods, etc? If an object was floating far out in space between the galaxies, far away from the force of gravity of the Sun, which type of motion would the object naturally pursue? This may help students express any preconceptions they have, such as the two listed above. (Newton's First Law states that if there is no unbalanced force on an object, it continues in its straight line motion, if it was initially moving, or it continues at rest, if it was initially at rest.)

Lesson 2: Balloon Rockets in Motion
The key concept in this lesson is Newton's Third Law: For every action there is an opposite and equal reaction. The air coming out of the balloon is the action. The balloon moving in the opposite direction is the reaction. Friction makes the rockets slow down and stop.

Lesson 3: Forces and Motion
Newton's Second Law states that an object will change its velocity of motion (accelerate) if an unbalanced force acts on it, and that the greater the force, the greater the change in motion or velocity it will experience. When students draw a diagram of the force on a rocket, for example, they should also indicate that friction backward is a force. If the force forward (the thrust of the rocket) and the force backward (the air friction) are equal, there should be two arrows of equal length in opposite directions. The rocket will then move at constant velocity. When thrust stops (e.g., the balloon runs out of air), the force of friction backward will quickly stop the rocket. All this is challenging for Grade 6 students to understand, and will involve a lot of questioning, prediction, and discussion of the Communicate questions.

Lesson 4: Pendulums
This activity provides opportunities for students to control variables in an experiment. Most students have the preconception that heavier objects always fall faster, and will think that the variable of mass will affect the swing of the pendulum. However, they will be surprised to find that this is not true. A heavier mass on the pendulum swings with the same frequency. It is important to first have the students predict their answer, so that all can see what preconceptions they have, and they can be surprised by the result. The arc length or amplitude of the pendulum swing also leaves the frequency unaffected, unless it is very large.

Lesson 5: Circles into Lines
The principal concept in this activity is the transfer of motion from linear to rotational through machines. In Grade 5, students may have studied the transfer of energy from one form to another in the unit Conservation of Energy. If some of your students draw an analogy with this concept, they are not far off!

Lesson 6: Friction Can Be a Drag!
Students don't naturally think of friction as a force. To them, a force is something external applied to the block, such as a spring scale. However, friction is also an external force applied to the block by the rough surface it rests on. It is important to establish friction as a force, acting backward on the block, so that students will understand that a forward force is only needed to maintain the motion of a block because a force of friction is pulling the block backward. Out in space, where there is no friction, no forward force is needed to keep something moving.

Lesson 7: Reducing Friction
This activity provides an opportunity to reinforce the concept of friction as a force.

Lessons 8, 9, and 10
Little research has been done on children's preconceptions of simple machines. However, this does not mean that they don't have any misconceptions. Good questioning and mind mapping will bring them out.

Lesson 11: Collisions
Most children have already associated "energy" with moving objects, so the idea that moving objects have kinetic energy is not new. They may have been introduced to this concept in the Grade 5 unit, Conservation of Energy.

Lessons 12, 13, and the Design Project
In these activities, students apply and extend the new concepts.

Opportunities for Ongoing Assessment

Activities throughout *Addison Wesley Science and Technology* provide opportunities to assess students on an ongoing basis. Here are some of the ways to assess and evaluate students as they work:

Students can be encouraged to keep a portfolio of work that they choose from the unit as they work through *Motion*. Portfolios provide useful evaluation tools to report to parents. The Assessment Follow-up at the end of each activity often suggests useful pieces for students to include in their portfolio.

Students' answers to questions in the Communicate section of the activities can be recorded in their science notebooks or placed in their portfolio. These answers provide clues to students' development of thinking of the science and technology involved in *Motion*. The Assessment Follow-up at the end of each activity often suggests Communicate questions that are particularly appropriate for assessment of specific expectations. This information can be recorded on an ongoing basis on Line Master 1: Ongoing Assessment Tracking Sheet.

Line Master 1 can be used to record student achievement throughout the unit. Using this chart, you can record ongoing student achievement of the three overall expectations of the unit and of students' abilities to communicate their learning. You can fill in this sheet in whatever way you feel comfortable, for example, using check marks, to indicate students have successfully met the expectations. An example of how to use this page is shown here.

You will notice that some activities have the following icons:

These activities provide opportunities to assess students' developing skills of inquiry and design. Students can use Line Masters 10: The Inquiry Process for Science and 11: The Design Process of Technology (found at the back of this module) to record their plans and responses to these activities.

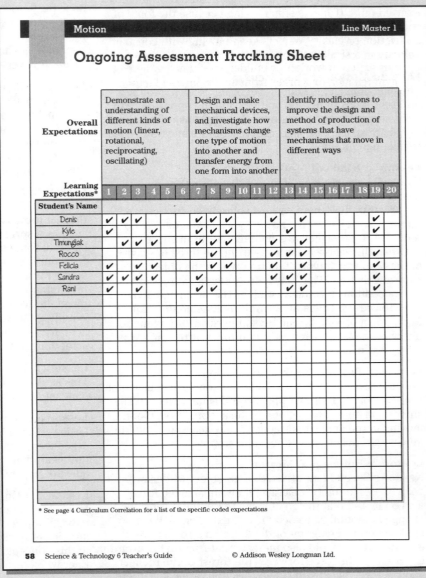

Line Master 1: Ongoing Assessment Tracking Sheet

Unit Overview

In this unit, students explore different types of motion. They will:

- demonstrate an understanding of different kinds of motion (linear, rotational, reciprocating, oscillating)
- design and make mechanical devices, and investigate how mechanisms change one type of motion into another and transfer energy from one form into another
- identify modifications to improve the design and method of production of systems that have mechanisms that move in different ways

Planning Notes

① **Classroom Visitors**
Invite guest speakers who have an interest in or whose work involves motion. You might invite a construction worker or builder, mechanic, athlete or gym teacher, or worker from an automated factory. Invite students to prepare some questions ahead of time.

② **Collecting Additional Materials**
Students will benefit from studying as varied a collection of materials that involve motion as possible. To add to the collection available, you may wish to ask students to bring in any items they have at home.

③ **Classroom Environment**
As they progress through the unit, students will be adding to a display of illustrations of motion. Arrange an appropriate, accessible place for the display in the classroom. If you have sufficient room, try to make the area resemble an art gallery display. Have file cards available for students to write their captions.

Non-print Resources

The following resources may be useful research tools for students.

Web sites:
Forces and Motion
http://www.stemnet.nf.ca/CITE/flightsc.htm

Rube Goldberg
http://rubegoldberg.com

CD-ROMs:
The Way Things Work. DK Multimedia, 1994 (WIN)

Launch: Motion at the Circus

1 class period

Assessing Students' Prior Knowledge

Post a large sheet of paper and divide it into 3 columns. Label these "Know," "Wonder," and "Learned." Explain that you are interested in facts, or things that students know to be true about motion. Ask, **What do you know about motion?**

Have students work individually at first, writing down everything they think they know about motion. Then ask them to read their responses to the class, while you record their statements on the KWL (Know, Wonder, Learned) chart under the heading "Know." Before you add each entry, ask the class whether they agree that the statement is true. If any students question whether a particular statement is true, reword that statement as a question and enter it in the "Wonder" column instead. Finally, ask students if they have any questions or things they would like to find out about motion, and write these responses in the "Wonder" column.

This KWL chart will be added to and edited throughout this unit. Post it where it can be easily reached and worked on.

Know	Wonder	Learned
- Motion uses energy and body parts - Animals show motion - Plants show movement - Vehicles, robots, appliances all have movement - Water and liquids have motion, as well as underwater creatures - The Earth moves - There is motion in nature, such as avalanches and tornadoes	- What is motion? - Why do things move? - What causes motion?	

• Focus on Literacy •

This is a good time to initiate an ongoing vocabulary/spelling list of "Motion" words. The list has three purposes: to aid comprehension of the text by providing students unfamiliar with new vocabulary with a quick reference, to encourage students to use new vocabulary in their writing and speaking, and to encourage students to use correct spelling of motion vocabulary. The list consists of four columns and should be completed with your students. It can be added to at the beginning of each activity, and used daily so that students become familiar with using the words.

Word	Picture or Symbol	Connected Words	Word in a Sentence
category		categorize	
elasticity		elastic	
gravity		grave (serious)	
mechanical		machine,	
device		mechanic	
collision		collide	
propel		propeller	

Introduce the Unit

Explain to students that they are about to study a unit on motion. Encourage students to bring any materials about motion they may already have at home. This could include books, magazines, etc., or toys and games that exhibit different types of motion. Students may know a mechanic, engineer, or scientist who could be a guest speaker for the class. Ask students for names and permission to contact these people. You can invite them or other specialists you may know to speak to the class. Alternatively, students could write to these people with their questions about motion.

Introduce the Design Project

Inform students that at the end of this unit, they will be designing their own machines. The machines will be a Rube Goldberg-type of invention that will perform a simple task. They will later present their design and invention to the class.

Through the Student Book

Have students form small groups to read the initial paragraph and then begin working on the Work On It section. Bring the class together after they have completed the questions to share their responses.

Students might find it easier to categorize the examples of motion in the circus picture if they write each motion on a small index card and then manipulate the cards to fit appropriate categories.

Communicate

Question 1: Student questions will vary. Examples may include:
- *Are there scientific names for the categories of motion?*
- *Why do things move?*

Revisit the KWL chart already established and posted. Ask, **What new questions do you have? What else would you like to find out?** Record any questions they offer in the "Wonder" column of the chart. Check them off as the answers are learned throughout the unit.

Build On What You Know

Have students begin collecting photographs or drawings of motion to create a class bulletin board. These pictures will be used throughout the unit. Have students decide how they want the display to look.

1 Kinds of Motion

1 class period

Skill Focus:
observing, comparing

Materials

No materials are required.

Optional Materials

- items to demonstrate motion, as illustrated in the student book (e.g., yo-yo, broom, fan, plunger, hammer)

Bookshelf

Macauley, David, *The Way Things Work* (Houghton Mifflin Co., 1988).

Learning Expectations

In this lesson students will:

> describe, using their observations, ways in which mechanical devices and systems produce a linear output from a rotary input (LE 1)

> use appropriate vocabulary, including correct science and technology terminology, in describing their investigation and observations (LE 10)

> communicate the procedures and results of investigations for specific purposes and to specific audiences (LE 12)

Lesson at a Glance

In this reading activity, students will learn the categories that science often uses to group types of motion. The four kinds of motion are linear motion, rotational motion, reciprocating motion, and oscillating motion. They will also see examples of each kind of motion and try to classify the motions in the Launch activity based on these categories.

Curriculum Connections

In this lesson, students have the opportunity to develop skills and concepts in these areas:

Mathematics:

Measurement
- relate time, distance, and speed: kilometres per hour

Social Studies:

Developing Inquiry/Research and Communication Skills
- formulate questions to serve as a guide to gathering information
- analyse, classify, and interpret information

Language Arts:

Reading
- summarize and explain the main ideas in information materials and cite details that support the main ideas
- select appropriate reading strategies
- use their knowledge of the elements of grammar and the structure of words and sentences to understand what they read
- understand specialized words or terms, as necessary
- use a variety of conventions of formal texts to find and verify information

Oral and Visual Communication
- speak correctly, observing common grammatical rules such as subject-verb agreement, noun-pronoun agreement, and consistency of verb tense

Science and Technology Background

Motion is often grouped into four categories based on similar characteristics. The four kinds of motion are:

- linear motion—motion along a straight line. A car moving along the road and a thrown baseball are examples of linear motion.
- rotational motion—motion along a curved path or in a circle. The wheels of a bicycle or a spinning Frisbee are examples of rotational motion.
- reciprocating motion—motion that alternates backwards and forwards in a linear motion. It is often linked through various devices to rotational motion. The pistons of an automobile and a self-inking stamp are examples of reciprocating motion.
- oscillating motion—motion of an object back and forth around a central point. A plucked guitar string and the pendulum of a clock are examples of oscillating motion.

Get Started

Through an Activity

Bring into class the objects in the pictures on Student Book page 4: a yo-yo, electric fan, hammer, broom, and toilet plunger. Show how each one works to demonstrate the motion that the photos are representing.

Through the Student Book

Have students read the Get Started paragraph individually. Ask, **Look at the objects on page 4. Can you describe how they are moving? Can you describe how these motions are similar to what you identified in the Launch activity? Which of the objects you see on page 4 have motion that is similar?**

Work On It SINGLE

Have students read the information on Student Book pages 5 and 6. Ask students to think of other examples of the different kinds of motion they see in their everyday lives. Ask, **Can you give me other examples of linear motion? rotational motion? reciprocating motion? oscillating motion?**

To help students think of other examples of the four kinds of motion, direct their attention to specific aspects of their lives: their own body movement, their home, the playground, the street, and amusement parks. Challenge students to show each type of motion with all or a part of their bodies. Two people may be needed to show reciprocating motion.

Discuss the last sentence of the last paragraph. Ask, **What do you think would happen if the right movement *did not* occur in the right place at just the right time?**

Communicate

Bring the class back together. Check their understanding by asking questions such as the following: **Why do you think it is good to group observations that we have, like we did for motion?** After students respond, explain that grouping is one way that we can study things. By studying a group that share similar characteristics, we can better understand them. Remember that there is no "right" way to group things. We group them so that they make sense to us.

Question 1: Student answers will vary. Students should describe the motions in their own words and give examples. Examples could be:

- *linear motion—a thrown ball or a moving car*
- *rotational motion—a Ferris wheel or the wheels of a moving bicycle*
- *reciprocating motion—a car piston or a locomotive's wheels (note that students may have difficulty identifying an example of reciprocating motion)*
- *oscillating motion—a swing or clock pendulum*

Question 2: Student answers will vary. Students could notice that there is a lot of linear and rotational motion. Wheels are used to move things—rotational motion creates linear motion.

Question 3: Skaters use linear motion when they glide along the ice and rotational motion when they spin.

Question 4: Student answers will vary. Examples may include:

- *linear motion—the tightrope walker or the monkey on the bicycle*
- *rotational motion—the unicycle wheel or the rolling acrobat*
- *reciprocating motion—no obvious examples*
- *oscillating motion—the trapeze or the bungee jumpers*

Two motions occur together in the unicycle (rotational motion of the wheels causes the unicycle to move in a linear fashion).

Build On What You Know

Student pictures can be added to the bulletin board and placed together with similar motions—linear, rotational, reciprocating, or oscillating. If there is more than one motion, have students decide which kind of motion is most obvious.

Extension

For Enrichment

Have students research the steam engine, one of the first examples of reciprocating motion in a machine.

Have students draw a picture of an amusement park. Next to each ride, have them indicate the kinds of motion involved in each ride. Is there more than one kind of motion involved in any rides?

For Reteaching

Bring the following, or similar, objects into the class to demonstrate the four kinds of motion:

- linear motion—toy car on a track, thrown ball
- rotational motion—bicycle tire, spinning top
- reciprocating motion—self-inking stamp, steam locomotive wheels
- oscillating motion—ball on the end of a rubber band, pendulum

After you have demonstrated each, have the students identify the kind of motion and explain their reason for placing it in that category. Some examples may demonstrate two or more kinds of motion.

Assessment Follow-up

Students' responses to the questions in Communicate will allow you to assess their ability to use appropriate vocabulary and terminology when categorizing and describing different types of motion (LE 10).

2 Balloon Rockets in Motion

1–2 class periods

Skill Focus:
observing, comparing, experimenting, inferring

Materials for each group

- oblong balloons
- 4-m string or nylon line
- drinking straw
- chair
- desk
- tape
- ruler or measuring tape
- timing device (optional)
- cardboard
- pencil
- scissors

Bookshelf

Morgan, Sally, *Movement* (Facts on File, 1993).

Learning Expectations

In this lesson students will:

> investigate ways of reducing friction so that an object can be moved more easily (LE 6)

> design and make mechanical devices that change the directions and speed of an input to produce a desired output and that perform a useful function (LE 7)

> use appropriate vocabulary, including correct science and technology terminology, in describing their investigation and observations (LE 10)

Lesson at a Glance

In this lesson, students learn about the causes of motion. They investigate linear and rotational motion using balloon rockets that either travel along a string or cause a round piece of cardboard to spin.

Curriculum Connections

In this lesson, students have the opportunity to develop skills and concepts in these areas:

Mathematics:
Measurement
- select the most appropriate standard unit to measure linear dimensions

Data Management and Probability
- make inferences and convincing arguments that are based on data analysis

Social Studies:
Developing Inquiry/Research and Communication Skills
- use appropriate vocabulary to describe their inquiries and observations

Language Arts:
Writing
- use the positive, comparative, and superlative forms of adjectives correctly

Reading
- make judgments and draw conclusions about ideas in written materials on the basis of evidence

- understand specialized words or terms, as necessary

Oral and Visual Communication
- use constructive strategies in small group discussions

- follow up on others ideas and recognize the validity of different points of view in group discussions or problem-solving activities

Science and Technology Background

Linear motion and rotational motion are the two most common kinds of motion that students find in their everyday lives. In linear motion, the force is applied to an object at its centre of mass. The centre of mass is

continued

the point in an object where its mass is equal in all directions. A force applied at this point causes the object to move in a straight line in the direction of the applied force.

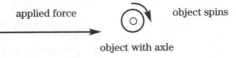

In rotational motion, the force is applied to an object at a point outside of its centre of mass. With this kind of force, the object spins in a circle around its centre of mass. More commonly, rotational motion occurs when the force is applied to an object at a point outside of its centre of mass and there is an axle placed at the centre of mass. This causes the object to spin on the axle.

applied force   object spins

object with axle

Get Started

Through an Activity

Blow up a balloon, twist the end closed, and hold it. Ask, **What is going to happen when I let this balloon go? What kind of motion could occur?**

After several students have given their hypotheses, let the balloon go.

Ask, **How could I get the balloon to have linear motion? How could I get rotational motion?**

Through the Student Book

Have students read the Get Started paragraph individually.

Ask students, **What do you think is the most common kind of motion you find in your everyday lives?** Students will probably say that linear motion is most common, but that they see rotational motion quite often as well. Explain that, in this lesson, they will be investigating two of the most common kinds of motion—linear motion and rotational motion.

Work On It

Organize the groups, making sure that the expectations for group work are clear. Some examples include:
- read the procedure first, before starting the activity
- share the work—everyone should participate
- be respectful of others
- stay on task

Since there are different skills involved in group work, choose one to focus on prior to starting the activity. For example, you might say: **As we move into our groups today, I'd like us to remember our group skills by making sure we address the people in our group by name, to listen actively, and to keep our hands and feet to ourselves.**

To help students share the work, assign roles to each student in the group. One person is the **reader**, who reads each instruction to the group. Another person is the **recorder**, who records the group's observations. A third person is the **reporter**, who reports the group's findings to the class. After the class is clear on their behaviour and your expectations, proceed with the Work On It part of the activity.

Remind students of the need to record their observations and measurements as they perform the investigation. You may wish to show them how to organize their observations in a chart.

Communicate

Bring the class together after they have read the assignment. Check their understanding by asking them, **What kind of motion is involved in each section of the activity?** (linear motion in the horizontal rocket and rotational motion in the circular rocket)

Question 1: The balloon rockets moved because of the force of the air moving out of the balloon.

The movement of the balloon is explained by Newton's Law of Motion: For every action, there is an equal and opposite reaction. As air rushes out of the balloon with a certain force, an equal amount of force pushes the balloon forward. This is how rockets are propelled into space.

Question 2: Friction caused the balloon rockets to slow down and then stop. The main causes of friction were the straw rubbing on the string, and the air resistance as the balloon flew along the string. When the balloon rocket had to go up, it also had gravity working against it.

Question 3: The balloon rockets moved faster or farther if there was more air moving out of the balloon, if the rocket was more oblong than round, or if it moved downward. More air creates more force, which leads to more motion, an oblong balloon creates less air resistance to slow the balloon, and moving downward lets gravity add to the forces causing motion.

Question 4: Student responses will vary. Air is used in the braking systems of some buses and trucks. This air pushes against the brake pads and causes them to move against the brake drum, slowing and stopping the vehicle. Air is also used in some tools. These tools are called pneumatic tools. They can cause a jackhammer to move up and down, create a force to drive a nail, or blow sand in a sand blasting machine. Windmills, which use wind to power machines to grind grain or pump water, are an early form of air-powered machines.

Extension

For Enrichment

Have students research the history of the rocket. How are the rockets they first made the same as the rockets that propel astronauts to the new International Space Station? How are they different?

Design Challenge

Use Activity Centre 1: The Ultimate Balloon Rocket! to challenge students to design a rocket that goes farthest along the string.

3 Forces and Motion

1–2 class periods

Skill Focus:
observing, comparing, classifying, inferring

Materials

No materials are required.

Bookshelf

Lafferty, Peter, *Force and Motion* (Stoddart Publishing Co., 1992).

Learning Expectations

In this lesson students will:

> use appropriate vocabulary, including correct science and technology terminology, in describing their investigations and observations (LE 10)

> communicate the procedures and results of investigations for specific purposes and to specific audiences (LE 12)

Lesson at a Glance

This lesson is a reading assignment that gives students background information about forces and motion, and the relationship between the two. Since this reading assignment introduces several new terms, you may wish to use a sort and predict pre-reading strategy.

Curriculum Connections

In this lesson, students have the opportunity to develop skills and concepts in these areas:

Mathematics:

Data Management and Probability
- make inferences and convincing arguments based on the analysis of tables, charts, and graphs

Social Studies:

Developing Inquiry/Research and Communication Skills
- analyse, classify, and interpret information
- formulate questions to serve as a guide to gathering information

Language Arts:

Reading
- make judgments and draw conclusions about ideas in written materials on the basis of evidence
- select appropriate reading strategies
- identify different forms of writing and describe their characteristics
- use their knowledge of the elements of grammar and structure of words and sentences to understand what they read
- use their knowledge of word origins and derivations to determine the meaning of unfamiliar words
- understand specialized words or terms, as necessary
- use punctuation to help them understand what they read

Oral and Visual Communication
- speak correctly, observing common grammatical rules such as subject-verb agreement, noun-pronoun agreement, and consistency of verb tense

3

Science and Technology Background

An understanding of the relationship between force and motion is fundamental to any study of motion. All new motion is caused by a force—a push or a pull. Any object that moves had to have a force act on it.

Force is referred to as a vector quantity. This means that not only is the value of a force important, the direction that the force acts is also important. You can push a table with a force, but the results of that force will depend on the direction that the force is applied. If the force is from above, the table will probably not do anything. However, if the force is from the side, and is strong enough, the table will move along the floor. The greater the force, the faster and/or farther the table will move.

A second important concept is that there are often several forces acting on an object at one time. If two forces acting on an object are in opposite directions and equal in strength, there is a balance of forces and no new motion is created. For example, a book sitting on a table has two forces acting on it. The force of gravity is trying to pull the book down, while the force of the table pushes back up and the book does not move. However, when one force acting on an object is greater than the other, the result is an unbalanced force, which leads to new motion. The direction of the greater force is the direction that an object will move. For example, when you push a box along the floor, you exert a force in the direction you are pushing. However, friction acts in the opposite direction to your force and tries to stop the motion. If your pushing force is greater than the force of friction, then the box will move.

Get Started

Through an Activity

Before starting, review the fact that gravity means that the earth pulls objects and people toward its centre. That's why we stay on the ground. Ask students, **If gravity is pulling us down, why don't we fall?** After students have had a chance to guess, explain that the forces in our leg muscles push us the other way against the force of gravity.

Engage a student in a tug of war using a rope. Explain the forces that are being applied and which force is greater at any instant. If you are winning the game, your force is greater. If both sides are pulling, but no one is winning, the forces are equal.

Through the Student Book

Have students read the Get Started paragraph individually.

Work On It SINGLE

One way to prepare students for a reading assignment is to use a sort and predict strategy. Have students work in pairs to complete the following activity. Then bring the class back together to share their responses.

Students write each word from the following list on a separate card, then sort the words into four or five categories. They name each category. There are no right or wrong categories, but students should be able to explain why they put the words into the categories they did.

This is an opportunity to assess student reading ability. As students are reading this piece, visit them and see how they approach the task of reading for information. Ask students to read a sentence or two aloud, then tell what the new piece of information is.

force	balanced	roller coaster	motion
arrows	faster	unbalanced	feather
upward	strength	bat	balloon
circle	equal	direction	baseball
push	gravity	parachute	opposite

When students have done their sorting, have them predict what they think the reading will be about. Ask, **What topics will you be investigating? List three or four questions that you want to have answered while you study this section.**

After students have done this activity, have them work individually to read the information on Student Book pages 9–10.

• Focus on Literacy •

Add new vocabulary with your students to the 4-column chart started in the Launch. Include words from this activity and the previous two activities.

Word	Picture or Symbol	Connected Words	Word in a Sentence
linkages		link in a chain	
principles			
pistons			
propels		propeller	
exerts		exertion	
balanced forces			
unbalanced forces			
linear		line	
rotational		rotate, rotation	
released		laisser (French)	
horizontal		horizon	
taut		tight	
launch		launch pad	
reciprocating		reciprocate	
oscillate		oscillation	

Communicate

Bring the class together after they have read the assignment. Check their understanding by drawing a picture of a hot air balloon and a picture of a person falling with a parachute. Ask, **What forces are acting in each case? Which force is greater?**

Question 1: Student answers will vary. Students could describe pedalling their bicycle, riding in the car, or walking along the road. Force diagrams would vary with each situation.

Question 2: Students' diagrams should include the balloon rocket and horizontal string.
a. The force of air caused the rocket to move.
b. The force of friction, the rubbing of the straw on the string, caused the rocket to stop moving.

c. The diagram can be confusing if students are unfamiliar with Newton's Third Law of Motion—for every action, there is an equal and opposite reaction. As air moves out of the balloon (the action), the balloon moves in the opposite direction (the reaction). This reaction force causes the movement of the balloon and causes the force diagram to have it's arrow head in the correct direction.

Question 3:

a. Student answers and diagrams will vary, but should show the person with the force of gravity acting to pull the person down. (Some students may recognize that air resistance will be acting in the opposite direction.) This unbalanced force leads to the motion of the person that causes him to fall.

b. Student answers and diagrams will vary, but should show the person with the force of gravity acting to pull the person down and an equal and opposite force caused by the bungee cord pulling up. This leads to a balanced force and no motion for the instant he is in that position. However, a short time later, the force the bungee cord creates is greater than the force of gravity and the person is pulled up again.

Question 4:

a. Student diagrams will vary, but should have equal length arrows pointing in opposite directions, each representing a different team. The forces are balanced and no motion occurs.

b. Student diagrams will vary, but should have the force arrow that represents the right-side team longer than the left-side team. This is an unbalanced force and the motion will be in the direction of the right-side team.

Question 5: Student answers will vary. Students could use the elastic force causing motion while jumping on the trampoline, various places where the force of gravity is working, elastic force of the bungee cords, or muscles causing people to move.

Build On What You Know

Student answers and diagrams will vary depending on the pictures they choose. Ask students to focus on the forces that lead to the motion of the pictures they choose.

Extension

For Enrichment

Have students research parachutes as an example of something that uses friction in a beneficial way (air resistance). They could investigate changes in parachutes, military versus sports parachutes, other uses of parachutes (e.g., space shuttle, dragster race cars), etc.

Have students compare force acting on a parachute and on a stationary hot air balloon, on an ascending hot air balloon, and on a descending hot-air balloon. How are they the same and how are they different?

Have students complete Activity Centre 2: All Fall Down! to experiment how the size of the parachute affects the speed of the fall.

Design Challenge

If students perform Activity Centre 2: All Fall Down! see if they can design a parachute that will slow the fall of the ball of clay enough to keep it from squashing when it lands.

4 Pendulums

1–2 class periods

Skill Focus:
*observing,
comparing,
experimenting,
inferring,
hypothesizing*

Materials for each group

- string
- scissors
- paper clips
- metal washers
- pencil
- 30-cm ruler
- stopwatch or watch with second hand

Bookshelf

Bender, Lionel, *Eyewitness Books – Invention* (Stoddart Publishing Co. Ltd., 1991).

Learning Expectations

In this lesson students will:

> plan investigations for some of these answers and solutions, identifying variables that need to be held constant to ensure a fair test and identify criteria for assessing solutions (LE 9)

> use appropriate vocabulary, including correct science and technology terminology, in describing their investigations and observations (LE 10)

> communicate the procedures and results of investigations for specific purposes and to specific audiences (LE 12)

> describe modifications that could improve the action of a variety of devices at home (LE 17)

Lesson at a Glance

In this lesson, students investigate one form of motion—oscillating motion—using a pendulum. They make a hypothesis about which variable will affect the time it takes a pendulum to make 15 complete swings, then test their hypothesis, and report their results.

Although the focus of this activity is oscillating motion, students also learn how an experiment should be organized. They are introduced to experiences with experimental variables and the use of controls.

Curriculum Connections

In this lesson, students have the opportunity to develop skills and concepts in these areas:

Mathematics:

Number Sense and Numeration
- identify the use of number in various careers

Data Management and Probability
- design surveys, organize the data into self-selected categories and ranges, and record the data on spreadsheets or tally charts

Concluding and Reporting
- recognize that different types of graphs can present the same data differently
- make inferences and convincing arguments based on the analysis of tables, charts, and graphs

Social Studies:

Developing Inquiry/Research and Communication Skills
- communicate information, using media works, oral presentations, written notes and descriptions, drawings, tables, charts, maps, and graphs

Language Arts:

Writing
- apply generalizations about spelling to identify exceptions to spelling patterns

Oral and Visual Communication
- use tone of voice and gestures to enhance the message and help convince or persuade listeners in conversations, discussions, or presentations

4

Oscillating motion is one form of motion. It is easy to identify because of its back-and-forth nature. In oscillating motion, an object moves one direction, then stops and moves back again, repeating in a regular pattern.

We can see oscillating motion in a lot of things all around that move back and forth. Even things too small to see, such as atoms, are moving back and forth. In some cases this motion is called a vibration. A vibration, like all oscillating motion, cannot exist in one instant, but needs time to move back and forth. If you hit a bell, the vibrations will continue for a time before they die down and eventually stop. If a student sits stationary on a swing without "pumping," the swing will eventually stop.

Pendulums swing back and forth at such a specific rate that they have long been used to control the motion of clocks. Galileo discovered, as the students will in this activity, that the time a free swinging pendulum takes to swing back-and-forth does not depend on the mass of the pendulum, or the arc of the swing, but only on the length of the pendulum string.

Get Started

Through an Activity

Ask students if they have ever seen a pendulum. If so, ask where and what its purpose was. Some students may have seen one in a grandfather clock and know that it is used to tell time.

Through the Student Book

Have students read the Get Started section. Ask if anyone knows how a pendulum is used to help keep time or why they are used on some clocks. Direct students to the last sentence in the introductory paragraph, and ask if they know what it means. List their ideas on chart paper and compare them later with their discoveries.

Work On It

Review what the students already know about how to study questions: how to form an hypothesis, how to test the hypothesis in a controlled experiment, how to collect and record data in an experiment, and how to draw a conclusion from the results.

Show the class an example of the pendulum set-up. Let the pendulum swing a few times and have the class count the number of swings. Invite student questions about how pendulums act. Ask for student volunteers to try different ways of moving the pendulum.

Remind the class of the purpose of the activity as described in the Get Started section: What factors affect the time it takes for a pendulum to make one swing?

Safety Caution

Make sure there is enough room between student groups for the activity to avoid student pendulums bumping each other.

How Does a Pendulum Swing?

Have students complete the first three steps of the procedure, then stop for a class discussion.

Do procedure step 4 as a class. List the possible reasons for different results in the activity. Students might think that the mass, the length of the string, or arc might all be factors.

Review the concept of the variable in an experiment—factors that affect the outcome of an experiment. Review the concept of controlling variables in an experiment—only one variable, or factor, can be tested at a time.

Students will see that you need to define what one swing will be. This is the first of five variables to be controlled. For this experiment, one swing will be when the washer moves away from you and back to the starting point. You will also need to determine what to do when the pendulum does not make a complete swing during the given time. Generally, if the pendulum is swinging away from you, you count the lower number of swings. If the pendulum has gone as far away from you as it can and has started back toward you, you count it as the next number. Point out that this is similar to rounding numbers, where over half is counted as the next number.

How Do the Variables Affect a Pendulum Swing?

This section of the procedure can be done using a jig-saw model. Assign one or two of the variables to be tested (mass, arc length, length of string, moving the pendulum) to each group. The groups then present their results to the class in the Communicate section.

In order to change only one variable, students must be consistent in holding the washer at a 45° or 90° angle. Encourage them to use a protractor to determine the correct angle.

Make sure that students understand that "check your prediction" at the end of each procedure means that they are expected to try out their prediction and record the results.

Communicate

Bring the class back together after they have completed testing their variables. Have each group present the results of their investigation to the class. Compare results of different groups that tested for the same variable. Were the results the same?

The results can be recorded on a class chart to aid comparison of group findings and also comparison with their original predictions.

Questions 1 and 2: Results should be as follows:
- mass—no difference between the number of swings using one or two washers
- arc length—no difference between the number of swings using 45° or 90° arc swings
- length of string—the longer the string, the fewer swings in 15 seconds
- moving the pendulum—In the previous activity, students learned that new motion is caused by force. In this case the students added a force to the pendulum motion by moving the pencil back and forth, and made a new motion.

Question 3: Student answers will vary, but may include pendulums in clocks, the swings on the playground, or some amusement park rides. Swings are a good example of a pendulum with a difference. Students may ask why, when they swing, the swing doesn't act exactly like the pendulums they investigated. The reason has to do with "pumping," where students move their bodies to cause the swing to go higher. This is similar to the variable of moving the pendulum in the experiment.

Students might need to look at pictures to help them think of examples of pendulums.

Question 4: Students could answer that the pendulum string could be made longer. This is actually what is done. There are controls to change the length of the pendulum in grandfather clocks to adjust their time.

Ask students to explain the reasons for their suggestions.

Extension

For Enrichment

Pendulums can be used to measure time accurately. Students can research how technology has changed the way we measure time and the accuracy of the measurements. Students could study ancient ways to keep time, such as water clocks, hour glasses, sundials, etc., as well as current methods, such as using the vibrations of quartz crystals.

Design Challenge

Students can use Activity Centre 3: Design Challenge: Make Time to design a pendulum that can measure exactly one minute.

5 Circles into Lines

1–2 class periods

Skill Focus:
observing, experimenting, making models

Materials for each group

- shoe box
- 6 flexible straws
- scissors
- paper
- tape
- ruler
- nails
- pen

Bookshelf

Ardley, Neil, *The Science Book of Machines* (Doubleday Canada Limited, 1992).

Macaulay, David, *The Way Things Work* (Boston: Houghton Mifflin Co., 1988).

Learning Expectations

In this lesson students will:

> describe, using their observations, ways in which mechanical devices and systems produce a linear output from a rotary input (LE 1)

> design and make mechanical devices that change the direction and speed of an input to produce a desired output and that perform a useful function (LE 7)

> use appropriate vocabulary, including correct science and technology terminology, in describing their investigations and observations (LE 10)

Lesson at a Glance

This lesson lets students build a device that converts rotary motion into linear motion. This conversion and its opposite (linear motion into rotary motion), which is sometimes called reciprocating motion, is used in a variety of mechanical devices such as automobile engines. It is also involved in rack and pinion steering, cams and cam followers, etc.

The procedure for this activity can be difficult. Practise the activity ahead of time to identify problem areas. The device you make can be used as a demonstration for students.

Curriculum Connections

In this lesson, students have the opportunity to develop skills and concepts in these areas:

Mathematics:
Measurement
- select the most appropriate standard unit to measure linear dimensions

Social Studies:
Developing Inquiry/Research and Communication Skills
- use appropriate vocabulary to describe their inquiries and observations

Language Arts:
Writing
- use verb tenses consistently throughout a piece of writing
- frequently introduce vocabulary from other subject areas into their writing

Reading
- make judgments and draw conclusions about ideas in written materials on the basis of evidence

Oral and Visual Communication
- use constructive strategies in small group discussions
- follow up on others ideas, and recognize the validity of different points of view in group discussions or problem-solving activities

Safety Caution

Students will be using a nail and scissors to make holes in cardboard. Remind students of the danger when using sharp implements. They should not have their hand, or other part of their body, on the opposite side of the cardboard when they pierce the hole.

5

Science and Technology Background

Reciprocating motion is really a combination of two other motions—rotational motion and linear motion—that are linked together in a way that one motion leads to the other. This kind of motion is found in various places of the automobile, as well as in other mechanical devices like the sewing machine.

The automobile crankshaft and piston assembly is a good place to see reciprocating motion in action. When the fuel in the cylinder burns, gases expand rapidly and force the piston down in the cylinder. This moves the connecting rod, which in turn moves the crankshaft in a circle, eventually causing the wheels of the car to turn. Thus, the up and down motion of the pistons causes the rotating motion of the crankshaft that drives the wheels of the car.

Get Started

Through an Activity

Remind students of earlier activities and the difficulties they may have had identifying examples of reciprocating motion. Explain that the reason for this is that reciprocating motion is actually a combination of two other motions—rotational motion and linear motion—that are linked together in a way that one motion leads to the other. This kind of motion is found in various places of the automobile, as well as in other mechanical devices like the sewing machine.

Through the Student Book

Have students read the Get Started paragraph. Ask if anyone has ever heard of the example suggested: pistons and crankshaft, rack and pinion steering, or any other reciprocating motion. If not, review the example of a car piston and crankshaft on Student Book page 5. Remind students that this is an example of a linked motion using linear motion and rotational motion. Ask, **What types of motion work together to form reciprocating motion in the automobile piston?**

Work On It

Before students begin on the procedure, show them the device you previously made as a demonstration. This will let them see what the finished project looks like.

Circulate among groups as they carry out the procedure, helping as necessary.

Communicate

Bring the class together after everyone is done building their device. Have several of the groups demonstrate how their device works.

Question 1: The motion in this machine is reciprocating motion. Students might be interested in learning that original cars were not started by a key, but rather by turning a crank handle at the front of the car. Pictures of this are available in books of antique cars.

Question 2: Student answers will vary. If the long strip was replaced with something stronger, you could move it up and down and the crank should turn.

Question 3: Student designs will vary. Students could use other materials to make a better device. To help students work in a logical, well-organized manner, have small groups first discuss their ideas, then draw and label their design, and then build the device.

Question 4: Student answers will vary. Students may realize that the sewing machine is very similar. The rotating motion causes the needle of the sewing machine to move up and down.

• Focus on Literacy •

To give students practice using motion vocabulary, students can work in groups to play a card game. On one side of an index card, write a word from your motion vocabulary chart. On the other side, write the meaning. To play, students spread the cards on the table with the meaning side up. Students in turn choose a card, read the meaning, and state what they think the word is. The group then checks to see if the student is correct. If the student is correct, he/she keeps the card. If not, the card is placed back on the table.

Extension

Design Challenge

Have students try to make a device that will have two strips moving up and down, such that when one is moving down, the other is moving up. What modifications to the original design are necessary?

6 Friction Can Be a Drag!

1–2 class periods

Skill Focus:
observing, comparing, interpreting, experimenting

Materials for each pair

- two identical blocks of wood with a hook in the end
- spring scale
- flat piece of wood
- piece of linoleum
- piece of carpet
- piece of cardboard

Bookshelf

The Jumbo Book of Science (Kids Can Press, 1994).

Learning Expectations

In this lesson students will:

> investigate ways of reducing friction so that an object can be moved more easily (LE 6)

> compile data gathered through investigation in order to record and present results (LE 11)

> communicate the procedures and results of investigations for specific purposes and to specific audiences (LE 12)

Lesson at a Glance

This lesson is an investigation into friction. Students will investigate the factors that influence friction—what causes it and, to a lesser extent, how they can decrease it. Students should begin to understand that friction works against motion and causes moving objects to slow down and eventually stop.

Curriculum Connections

In this lesson, students have the opportunity to develop skills and concepts in these areas:

Mathematics:
Number Sense and Numeration
- demonstrate ratio
- solve simple rate and ratio problems

Social Studies:
Developing Inquiry/Research and Communication Skills
- use appropriate vocabulary to describe their inquiries and observations
- construct and read a variety of graphs, charts, diagrams, maps, and models for specific purposes

Language Arts:
Writing
- frequently introduce vocabulary from other subject areas into their writing
Reading
- select appropriate reading strategies
- use generalizations about spelling to help pronounce words
Oral and Visual Communication
- use a varied vocabulary and a range of sentence structures to add interest to their remarks

Science and Technology Background

Friction is a force that resists motion. It works in the direction opposite to motion to slow a moving object down and eventually to stop it. Air resistance is one kind of friction. Students saw this kind of friction when they built their balloon rockets in Activity 2. There is also friction in wheels that slows rotational motion.

continued

There are two kinds of friction: static friction that keeps an object from starting to move, and kinetic friction that works against a moving object. It is more difficult to start an object moving than to keep it moving, so that static friction is greater than kinetic friction. Both kinds of friction occur because of bumps and irregularities in the surfaces of objects that are touching. Even very smooth surfaces have microscopic bumps on them. In general, the rougher the surface of an object, the more friction there is.

Friction is usually not helpful because it works against motion. It takes more force to move the object because of friction. But sometimes we use it if we want to stop motion, for example, in the brakes of a bicycle.

Get Started

Through an Activity

Have students rub their hands together. Ask, **What do you notice about your hands when you rub them together?** (They get hot.) **What causes the heat?** (Friction.)

Wind up a toy car and let it move across the floor or table. Ask, **Why did the car stop moving?** Students may respond that the spring wound down or that there is friction. Ask students if they have heard of the term friction and whether they know what it means.

Through the Student Book

Have students read the Get Started paragraph individually and look at the accompanying pictures. Ask, **How is friction involved in these pictures?** (The brakes on the bicycle use friction to stop.)

Work On It

Students work in pairs to complete this activity. Before they begin, remind students to create a chart in their notebooks like the one on Student Book page 17. Advise them that this chart will help them collect their data in the experiment.

Have students read the procedure for the experiment. To facilitate their understanding of what is required in an effective experiment, ask, **What variables are we going to investigate in this activity?** (What are the effects of certain variables—the kind of surface, the weight of the object, and the surface area—on friction when you pull a block?) **How are you going to test each variable?** (The investigation has students pull a block of wood across different surfaces, then two blocks, and then the block on its edge.)

It is important for students to keep the strength of their pull on the spring scale constant. If spring scales are not available, use a thick rubber band cut once to make a strip. Mark off the unstretched band with a pen in centimetres. Students can roughly determine the force by how much a given measurement (e.g., 6 cm) stretches.

Assessing Students at Work

This activity provides a chance for you to observe whether students can identify and control variables. Do they understand that they can only change one thing for each test they carry out?

• Focus on Literacy •

Add new vocabulary to the ongoing class chart with your students.

Communicate

Bring the class together after they have completed the assignment. Check their understanding by having groups share the results of their investigation. Ask students, **What conclusions can you make based on your findings?** Student answers will vary, but they could say that smoother surfaces have less friction.

Question 1: Student diagrams may vary. They should have an applied or pulling force that is greater than the force of friction. Because the block of wood moves, there is an unbalanced force.

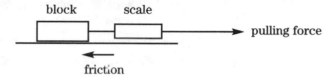

Question 2: Student answers may vary, depending on the materials used. From highest to lowest friction, the surfaces would likely be: carpet, cardboard, wood, linoleum.

Question 3: Student answers may vary. Students could test the friction of other surfaces such as cloth, smooth wood and rough wood, metal, dirt, grass, asphalt, glass, etc. In general, the smoother the surface, the less friction. Students could also test a sheet of ice by freezing water on a cookie sheet. This could lead to a discussion of winter driving and ice skating.

Question 4: Student predictions may vary. If three blocks are used, it would take approximately three times the force to move them along the surface. Similarly, it would take approximately four times the force to move four blocks.

Question 5: Student answers may vary. Students could put water (easy to test) or oil (messy to test) on the surface or wheels under the block to see if that would reduce friction and make the block easier to move.

Question 6: Student answers may vary. Friction on the brakes of an automobile and air resistance when they ride a bicycle are two examples students could use.

Question 7: Student answers may vary. Students could identify the friction between the straw and string and air resistance as friction in the horizontal balloon rocket.

Extension
For Enrichment
Students can use Activity Centre 4: Return of the Balloon Rocket to investigate how the type of string affects the amount of friction produced on a balloon rocket.

7

Reducing Friction

1–2 class periods

Skill Focus:
interpreting, observing

Materials

No materials are required.

In this lesson students will:

> demonstrate awareness that friction transforms kinetic energy into heat energy (LE 5)

> investigate ways of reducing friction so that an object can be moved more easily (LE 6)

> communicate the procedures and results of investigations for specific purposes and to specific audiences (LE 12)

> compare qualitatively the effort required to move a load a given distance using different devices and systems (LE 19)

Lesson at a Glance

This lesson is a reading assignment that follows up on the previous investigation of friction. In the previous activity, students looked at the factors that affect friction. In this reading assignment, they learn how friction works and what we can do to reduce it.

Curriculum Connections

In this lesson, students have the opportunity to develop skills and concepts in these areas:

Social Studies:

Developing Inquiry/Research and Communication Skills
- use appropriate vocabulary to describe their inquiries and observations
- formulate questions to serve as a guide to gathering information
- analyse, classify, and interpret information

Language Arts:

Reading
- summarize and explain the main ideas in information materials and cite details that support the main ideas
- make judgments and draw conclusions about ideas in written materials on the basis of evidence
- select appropriate reading strategies
- plan a research project and carry out the research
- use their knowledge of the elements of grammar and the structure of words and sentences to understand what they read
- use generalizations about spelling to help them pronounce words
- consult a dictionary to confirm pronunciation and/or find the meaning of unfamiliar words
- understand specialized words or terms, as necessary
- use a variety of conventions of formal texts to find and verify information

Oral and Visual Communication
- speak correctly, observing common grammatical rules such as subject-verb agreement, noun-pronoun agreement, and consistency of verb tense

7

The last activity gave an introduction to friction. This reading assignment follows up on the investigation and gives more information.

There are many ways to reduce friction. The first is to smooth the surface. If you slide an object on a smooth surface, there is less friction. Another way to reduce friction was discovered by ancient humans when they invented the wheel. Objects will roll easier than they will drag. We apply this principle through bearings, round metal balls that allow objects to move against each other easier.

Another way to reduce friction is through the use of lubricants. A lubricant works by providing a smooth covering over parts that move against each other. Oil, grease, and graphite are common lubricants.

Air resistance is a form of friction where the air works against an object in motion. One way to reduce this form of friction is to change the shape of the object in motion. Sleek, pointed objects have less air resistance than flat, blunt objects. The study of how the shape of an object affects the flow of air against it is called aerodynamics.

Get Started

Through an Activity

Ask students, **Do you think that friction is good or bad?** Help students understand that it depends on the situation. In some places, such as the brakes of a bicycle or a car, friction is good. However, in the car's engine, friction reduces motion and means more energy is needed.

Ask students, **What did you learn about friction in the last activity?** Students should remember that friction depends on the materials that are moving next to each other. **Are there any ways to reduce friction?** Students may already know about oil or other lubricants, or even about changing their position on their bicycle to make themselves more aerodynamic to reduce air resistance.

Through the Student Book

Ask students to predict what this activity is about by reading the title. Have students read the Get Started paragraph individually. Answer any questions students may have.

Assessing Students at Work

This activity provides a chance for you to observe whether students can read for understanding. As they read sections, ask questions about content.

Work On It SINGLE

Have students read the information on Student Book pages 19 and 20. Ask students who have difficulty with comprehension to explain individual sentences or paragraphs in their own words. Bring in examples of ways to reduce friction, such as a skateboard with bearing wheels, and several different lubricants. After students have read the information, show them the examples.

To demonstrate the principle of air resistance in paragraph 5, drop a sheet of paper to the floor at the same time as you drop a sheet of paper rolled into a ball. Which one has more air resistance?

To help students understand paragraph 6, look at pictures or models of airplanes, airplane wings, racing cars, and racing bicycle helmets. They all have a similar teardrop shape that cuts down on air resistance.

Communicate

Bring the class together after they have read the assignment. Check their understanding by asking, **What are the ways that you can use to reduce friction?** (Bearings, lubricants, change shape to reduce air resistance.) **When is friction good?** (When you want to stop motion.) **When is friction bad?** (When you want to move.)

Question 1: Student answers will vary. Students could identify bicycle brakes, automobile brakes, cleats on soccer shoes, sand on icy highways, etc. as ways that friction is helpful.

Question 2: Student answers will vary. Students could identify moving parts in an automobile engine, air resistance when they ride their bikes, and a slippery field when it is wet as ways that friction is not needed. To reduce this friction, you can add better lubricants to the engine, crouch to change shape on the bicycle, and wear cleats on the field.

Question 3: Student drawings and answers will vary, but should demonstrate that, once the parachute is opened, it creates more air resistance to slow the person's fall. It is an unbalanced force with gravity pulling down and air resistance working in the opposite direction.

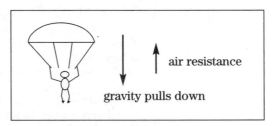

air resistance

gravity pulls down

Question 4: The curved pieces are used to reduce air resistance as the truck moves down the highway.

Build On What You Know

Student answers will vary. They might suggest changing the shape of objects, or the use of lubricants or bearings to reduce friction. Other choices can lead to an increase in friction.

Extension

For Enrichment

Have students research the ways that automobile makers reduce air resistance. Have them create a simple demonstration of how air resistance slows a car.

Have students research the ways that oil and lubrication manufacturers reduce friction.

Have a bicycle racer speak to the class. One focus could be how racers decrease air resistance when racing.

8 Simple Machines

1–2 class periods

Skill Focus:
observing, inferring, hypothesizing

Materials for each group

- block of wood with hook on it
- several other blocks of wood
- long thin pieces of wood
- spring scale
- a pile of books (4 or 5)
- smooth board for a ramp
- several pulleys
- string
- gears
- wheel and axle
- straws
- bamboo skewers
- a metre stick
- 2 chairs
- tape

Optional Materials

- saw
- drill
- hammer
- nails

Safety Caution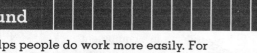

Remind students to be careful when using sharp or heavy equipment. Ensure they wear safety goggles and protective gloves, when necessary.

Learning Expectations

In this lesson students will:

> - communicate the procedures and results of investigations for specific purposes and to specific audiences (LE 12)
> - compare qualitatively the effort required to move a load a given distance using devices and systems (LE 19)

Lesson at a Glance

Students investigate ways that simple machines can be combined to perform the task of moving a block of wood to the top of a pile of books with the least amount of force possible.

The activity is an open-ended inquiry because there is no prescribed way to perform the task. Students will use previous knowledge of simple machines to solve the task. During the activity, students may discover new ways to use simple machines and will learn that certain combinations of simple machines are more effective in moving the block to the top of the pile of books than others.

Curriculum Connections

In this lesson, students have the opportunity to develop skills and concepts in these areas.

Mathematics

Geometry and Spatial Sense
- estimate the size of angles within a reasonable range
- recognize and describe in mathematical language the occurrence and application of geometric properties and principles in the everyday world

Language Arts:

Writing
- use subordinate clauses correctly
- use verb tenses consistently throughout a piece of writing
- frequently introduce vocabulary from other subject areas into their writing

Reading
- consult a dictionary to confirm pronunciation and/or find the meaning of unfamiliar words

Oral and Visual Communication
- use constructive strategies in small group discussions
- follow up on others ideas, and recognize the validity of different points of view in group discussions or problem-solving activities

Science and Technology Background

A machine is a device that helps people do work more easily. For example, you can use a car jack to help you lift a car that you could otherwise not lift. A machine performs at least one of the following functions:
- A machine may transfer forces from one place to another. For

continued

example, the chain of a bicycle transfers force from the pedals to the rear wheel.
- A machine may change the direction of a force. For example, a rope thrown over the branch of a tree can be used to lift a box.
- A machine may multiply speed or distance. For example, different-sized gears on a bicycle can be used to make it go faster.
- A machine may multiply force. For example, a lever can be used to increase the force needed to pry open a can.

All machines, no matter how complicated, are made of one or more of the six simple machines: inclined plane, pulley, wedge, screw, lever, or wheel-and-axle.

Get Started

Through an Activity

Begin with a brainstorming session. Ask students, **What do you know about machines? What do machines do?** As students suggest various responses, help them see that machines serve to make work easier.

Through the Student Book

After reading the text, ask students to give an example of where they have seen each simple machine. Ask students if they can match each simple machine shown in the pictures on the bottom of Student Book page 21 (inclined plane, pulley, wedge, screw, lever, wheel-and-axle).

• Focus on Literacy •

Add new vocabulary to the ongoing class chart with your students:

Word	Picture or Symbol	Connected Words	Word in a Sentence
transfer		trans=across	
inclined plane		inclination	
wedge			
lever		leverage	
wheel and axle			
screw			
transform		transformation	
pulley		pull	

Work On It

Begin the activity by telling students that humans have used machines to let them do tasks that otherwise seemed impossible. For example, the ancient Egyptians used simple machines to carve and move large blocks of stone to make the pyramids. Ask students, **How could the Egyptians have done this without the equipment we have today such as cranes and other machines?** Students may suggest that they could have used wedges to break stone, and various other simple machines—inclined planes, levers, wheel-and-axle—to move the blocks into place

To ensure that students have a good understanding of the six simple machines, make six columns on chart paper, each headed with a type of simple machine. Under each heading, list in words or pictures examples of that type of simple machine.

Assessing Students at Work

Since this is a laboratory investigation, use the opportunity to check for inquiry and design skills (including the safe use of tools, equipment, and materials). Did students use equipment, such as the scissors, correctly? Did the students apply the required skills and strategies to solve the problem?

8

Inform students that the activity they are about to do has no right way to do it. They are going to investigate ways to move a wooden block to the top of a pile of books using the same methods that the ancient Egyptians did.

As students begin to work through the procedure, you may want to assign responsibilities to each group member. For example:
- Project Manager—to oversee the entire project
- Materials Manager—to organize the collection and management of equipment and supplies
- Design Manager—to prepare the designs
- Communications Manager—to develop a report/display/ demonstration of the completed project

To ensure that the brainstorming required in step 2 of the procedure is done correctly, discuss and list the rules of brainstorming:
a. Record all ideas suggested by group members. Ideas can be recorded in words and/or sketches. Negative comments are never made.
b. Only when the group members have stopped suggesting ideas are specific ones chosen and tried.

You might want to role-play a brainstorming session with the whole class before the groups start to work. The class could consider something like "How would you weigh an elephant?"

Communicate

At the end of the activity, you may want to have groups demonstrate for the class the way that they discovered to move the block of wood with the least amount of force.

Ask, **Are there any similarities about the designs that used the least amount of force to move the block? How could other materials be used to make the designs better? Which simple machines were used most and how were they used in this activity?**

Question 1: Student answers will vary. Designs could include several simple machines that are linked to decrease forces. For example, students could have used an inclined plane, a wheel-and-axle, and a pulley system to move the block to the top of the books.

Question 2: Student answers will vary. Students may feel that stronger materials, such as wood or metal, would make a better device. Also, better wheel-and-axle or pulleys could improve the design by decreasing friction.

Question 3: Student answers will vary. Students could say that simple machines make the work easier, use less force. But they could also see that the machines become very complex and require you to move objects a greater distance. For example, in a complex pulley system, the string is pulled a longer distance to compensate for a decreased force.

Extension

For Enrichment

Have students research the techniques used in constructing the pyramids, Stonehenge, the Great Wall of China, and large monuments constructed in pre-industrial times. What simple machines did they use? Have students report their findings.

9 Levers

1–2 class periods

Skill Focus:
observing, comparing, inferring, experimenting, communicating

Materials for each group

- metre stick
- set of small masses
- fulcrum (wooden block)
- supporting wire or string loops
- 200-g mass
- spring scale
- 3 books
  (to stand the fulcrum on)
- tape

Learning Expectations

In this lesson students will:

> describe, using their observations, the purposes or uses of three classes of simple levers (LE 2)

> demonstrate an understanding of how linkages (systems of levers) transmit motion and force (LE 3)

> use appropriate vocabulary, including correct science and technology terminology, in describing their investigations and observations (LE 10)

> communicate the procedures and results of investigations for specific purposes and to specific audiences (LE 12)

> describe how different devices and systems have been used by different cultures to meet similar need (LE 20)

Lesson at a Glance

This lesson is about levers. Students investigate the three classes of levers and determine the ways that each is used.

Curriculum Connections

In this lesson, students have the opportunity to develop skills and concepts in these areas:

Mathematics:

Measurement
- use prefixes in the metric system correctly
- determine the relationship between milligrams, grams, and kilograms

Data Management and Probability
- organize the data into self-selected categories and ranges, and record the data on spreadsheets or tally charts
- experiment with a variety of displays of the same data using computer applications, and select the type of graph that best represents the data
- recognize that different types of graphs can present the same data differently
- make inferences and convincing arguments based on the analysis of tables, charts, and graphs

Social Studies:

Developing Inquiry/Research and Communication Skills
- use appropriate vocabulary to describe their inquiries and observations
- formulate questions to serve as a guide to gathering information
- construct and read a variety of graphs, charts, diagrams, maps, and models for specific purposes
- communicate information, using media works, oral presentations, written notes and descriptions, drawings, tables, charts, maps, and graphs

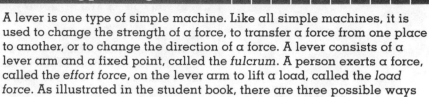

Science and Technology Background

A lever is one type of simple machine. Like all simple machines, it is used to change the strength of a force, to transfer a force from one place to another, or to change the direction of a force. A lever consists of a lever arm and a fixed point, called the *fulcrum*. A person exerts a force, called the *effort force*, on the lever arm to lift a load, called the *load force*. As illustrated in the student book, there are three possible ways that a lever can be arranged, each of which is useful in different situations:

- In a first class lever, the fulcrum is placed between the point where the effort is exerted and the load. A seesaw is an example of a first class lever. If the distance from the fulcrum to the effort force is greater than the distance from the fulcrum to the load, the effort force will be less than the load. The lever has increased the strength of the force.
- In a second class lever, the fulcrum is at one end of the lever arm, the point where the effort is exerted is at the other end, and the load is in between. A wheelbarrow is an example of a second class lever. It takes less effort force than load force to lift a load using a second class lever.
- In a third class lever, the fulcrum is at one end of the lever arm, the load is at the other, and the effort force is in between. A pair of tongs is an example of a third class lever.

Get Started

Through an Activity

Place a can of paint, a penny, and a screwdriver on the table. Say to students, **I need to pry the lid off this can of paint. Which will make the job easier, the penny or the screwdriver? Why?** Help students to understand that both the penny and the screwdriver can be used as levers, but because the screwdriver is longer, it makes the job easier.

Through the Student Book

Have students read the Get Started paragraph individually. Teach students how to pronounce Archimedes. Students might be interested in learning about the story of his discovery of water displacement when he was taking a bath, and about his invention of the Archimedes screw, which was used to raise water from a lower source.

Have examples of each of the three classes of levers to demonstrate how each one works. Show the relationship between the fulcrum, load force, and effort force in each.

Ask students to suggest examples of other levers they have seen. Students may suggest using a claw hammer to remove a nail, or a spatula to flip pancakes. Others may recognize that some of the joints in their bodies use levers.

Work On It

Depending on the time and resources available, this activity can be done with each group investigating only one class of lever and then sharing the information, or each group can perform all parts and the information can be compared at the end of the activity.

Have students read all the procedure steps carefully before they begin. Advise them that they should think carefully about the data they will need to collect. Ask, **What kind of data table could you use? Remember that a data table will help you collect and organize your data for use later.**

Students may need help in setting up a record sheet that includes spaces for predictions, observations, and sketches. Students should understand that it is important to record predictions so that comparisons can be made with their observations.

Ask students, **What variables are we going to investigate in this activity?** (What is the effect of the location of the fulcrum, load force, and effort force on the effort force needed to move a load?) **How are you going to test this?**

If necessary, demonstrate how the materials can be combined to make the three classes of lever.

As students carry out the investigation, help individual student groups as necessary. Make sure that students record any measurements of distance or force in their diagrams. This will allow them to share their information with other groups or to compare their results.

• Focus on Literacy •

To give students practice with motion vocabulary, have groups create a Context Clues game. Each group chooses 10 or more words from the chart and writes each word on a small card. On a sheet of chart paper, the group writes a sentence for each word, but draws a line where the word would be. The object of the game is to use the context of the sentence to figure out the missing word. Once the games are completed, they can be rotated to other groups or given to other classes as challenges.

Communicate

Bring the class together after they have read the assignment. Check their understanding by asking, **What is the use and purpose of each class of lever?**

Student answers should include the following:
- first class lever—changes force necessary to move load. You can use gravity to help push down to lift the load. You push down on the lever to lift a load.
- second class lever—changes force necessary to move load. You lift the lever to lift a load, but it takes a larger movement of the effort to move the load a smaller distance.
- third class lever—changes force necessary to move load, but you use more force to move it. Small movement of the effort moves the load a larger distance.

Question 1: Student answers will vary. Have students focus on the location of the fulcrum, load, and effort in each class of lever, as well as the results of each investigation.

Question 2: The load would have to be as close as possible to the fulcrum. Also, the lever arm would have to be very long.

Question 3: The load should be placed as close as possible to the wheel, which acts as a fulcrum.

Assessment Follow-up

Students' answers to Communicate questions 1–4 will allow you to assess their ability to describe the purposes or uses of three classes of simple levers (LE 2).
Communicate question 5 allows students to describe how different devices and systems have been used by different cultures (LE 20).

Question 4: The effort force is never less than the load force in a third class lever. This class lever is beneficial when small movements of the effort is necessary to move the load a great distance. The human arm and most cranes benefit from this arrangement.

Question 5: Student diagrams will vary. The shadoof is an example of a first class lever that has a heavy counterweight on one end and the bucket of water on the other. By having the counterweight adding an additional force of gravity, the force necessary to lift the bucket is less.

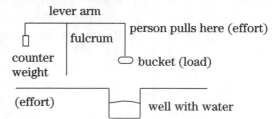

Question 6: Student diagrams will vary. The biceps are an example of a third class lever.

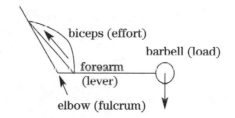

Build On What You Know

Students may find many examples of levers. They could include the body, a baseball player swinging a bat, a construction crane, or a playground seesaw.

Extension

For Reteaching

Sometimes students need to feel the differences in forces that different levers and fulcrum placement create. Bring a one metre plank board into the classroom. Place it on a low brick to create a first class lever. Place a large brick or other weight on one end and have students push down on the other end. Where do they place the fulcrum to lift the weight with as little effort as possible? Have students experiment with second and third class levers using the same materials.

For Enrichment

In a free exploration time, have students try lifting heavier loads with the smallest possible force, as suggested in Communicate question 2.

Design Challenge

Use Activity Centre 5: Design Challenge: The Tree House to challenge students to apply their knowledge of what they have learned about simple machines to solve the problem of raising a collection of materials up a tree.

10 Combining Simple Machines

1–2 class periods

Skill Focus:
observing, comparing

Materials for each pair

- various household items such as a bicycle, can opener, nut cracker, scissors, wind-up toy car, eggbeater, corkscrew, and so on

Learning Expectations

In this lesson students will:

> demonstrate an understanding of how linkages transmit motion and force (LE 3)

> compile data gathered through investigation in order to record and present results (LE 11)

> communicate the procedures and results of investigations for specific purposes and to specific audiences (LE 12)

> describe modifications that could improve the action of a variety of devices at home (LE 17)

> show an understanding of the impact of moving mechanisms on the environment and on living things (LE 18)

> describe how different devices and systems have been used by different cultures to meet similar needs (LE 20)

Lesson at a Glance

This lesson provides an opportunity for students to investigate the ways that simple machines—lever, screw, inclined plane, wedge, wheel-and-axle, and pulley—can be combined to make more complex machines. It is an excellent way for students to show the learning that they have acquired in the previous activities.

Curriculum Connections

In this lesson, students have the opportunity to develop skills and concepts in these areas:

Mathematics:
Data Management and Probability
- make inferences and convincing arguments based on the analysis of tables, charts, and graphs

Social Studies:
Developing Inquiry/Research and Communication Skills
- use appropriate vocabulary to describe their inquiries and observations
- formulate questions to serve as a guide to gathering information
- communicate information, using media words, oral presentations, written notes and descriptions, drawings, tables, charts, maps, and graphs

Language Arts:
Writing
- use subordinate clauses correctly
- use a colon before a list
- frequently introduce vocabulary from other subject areas into their writing

Reading
- summarize and explain the main ideas in information materials and cite details that support the main ideas
- select appropriate reading strategies
- plan a research project and carry out the research
- understand specialized words or terms, as necessary

Oral and Visual Communication
- speak correctly, observing common grammatical rules, such as subject-verb agreement, noun-pronoun agreement, and consistency of verb tense

Safety Caution

Caution students about any dangers associated with objects used in this activity. For example, caution students where they could get their fingers pinched with investigating an object like a nut cracker or can opener.

- use constructive strategies in small group discussions
- follow up on others ideas, and recognize the validity of different points of view in group discussions or problem-solving activities

Science and Technology Background

Machines are a part of our everyday life. Even the most complex machines are usually composed of several simple machines—lever, screw, inclined plane, wedge, wheel-and-axle, and pulley—combined into one larger machine. These machines are used to make our lives easier.

Get Started

Through an Activity

Review what students have already learned about machines. Invite students to name the six types of simple machines, and to identify what all machines have in common (i.e., they make work easier).

Through the Student Book

Have students read the Get Started paragraph individually. Summarize the concept that all complex machines are made of a combination of simple machines. As an example, hold up a stapler and ask students to identify which simple machines a stapler contains (the handle is a lever and the staples are wedges).

Work On It PAIR

This activity can be organized as a centres approach, with activity tables set up around the room and a different device or household item at each centre.

Remind students to read all the procedure steps carefully before beginning the activity. Suggest to students that they create a table in their notebooks like the one on Student Book page 28.

As students carry out the investigation, help individual student groups as necessary. You may draw their attention to some simple machines that might be less obvious in each device.

Communicate

Bring the class together after they have completed the assignment. Check their understanding by asking about the simple machines found in each complex machine. Ask different students to identify and describe the simple machines they saw.

Question 1: Student answers will vary. Levers are used often because of their ability to increase force and make work easier. Levers are found in a bicycle, can opener, nut cracker, scissors, etc.

Question 2: Student answers will vary. In a can opener, the lever handle transfers the force to the wheeled wedge that pierces the lid of the can, rotates on a screw, and opens the can.

Question 3: Student answers will vary. Students may suggest that the levers that operate the bicycle brakes could be longer to make them easier to apply forces.

Question 4: The nail clippers are a complex lever system. They are made up of a second and third class lever combined.

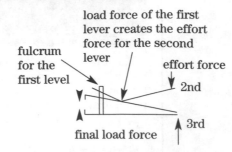

Question 5: Student answers will vary. Bicycles are made up of several simple machines, making them excellent for transportation. They use levers to multiply forces to make the pedals and wheels go around, they use wheels that are easy to turn, etc. Their limitations are their use up very steep hills, their reliance on fitness of the rider, and problems using them in some weather conditions like snow and cold.

Question 6: Student answers will vary. The wide treads for driving and steering keep them on top of the snow. However, as they travel on top on the snow, it is possible to damage the plants under the snow. Also, some people who travel on snowmobiles deliberately chase wildlife or cause destruction to plant life. Snowmobiles burn fossil fuels, and may leak oil into the environment.

Build On What You Know

Students should be able to find many pictures of mechanical devices that have simple machines. Help them to identify the simple machines in each. There is often one or two simple machines that have a major function in the operation of the machine. Have students focus on the obvious simple machines but also include other, less obvious ones. For example, most complex machines have screws to hold them together, and they play an important part in the ability of the machine to operate.

Extension

For Enrichment

Invite students to bring in additional household items or research other complex machines and report on the simple machines that comprise them. For example, what simple machines are used in the Canadarm on the space shuttles?

Have a automobile mechanic talk to your class about the simple machines that are involved in the automobile.

11 Collisions

1–2 class periods

Skill Focus:
observing, comparing, experimenting

Materials for each pair

- 30-cm plastic ruler with a centre groove or similar object
- 7 identical marbles
- book

Learning Expectations

In this lesson students will:

> demonstrate awareness that a moving mass has kinetic energy that can be transferred to a stationary object (LE 4)

> use appropriate vocabulary, including correct science and technology terminology, in describing their investigation and observations (LE 10)

> communicate the procedures and results of investigations for specific purposes and to specific audiences (LE 12)

Lesson at a Glance

This lesson covers kinetic energy and how it is transferred during collisions. Students investigate kinetic energy in collisions by rolling a marble in the groove of a ruler and colliding it with other stationary marbles.

Curriculum Connections

In this lesson, students have the opportunity to develop skills and concepts in these areas:

Mathematics:

Number Sense and Numeration
- pose problems involving whole numbers, decimals, and percents, and solve them using the appropriate calculation method: pencil and paper, or calculator, or computer

Measurement
- relate time, distance, and speed: kilometres per hour
- determine the relationship between milligrams, grams, and kilograms

Social Studies:

Developing Inquiry/Research and Communication Skills
- use appropriate vocabulary to describe their inquiries and observations
- formulate questions to serve as a guide to gathering information
- communicate information, using media works, oral presentations, written notes and descriptions, drawings, tables, charts, maps, and graphs

Language Arts:

Reading
- understand specialized words or terms, as necessary

Oral and Visual Communication
- use a varied vocabulary and a range of sentence structures to add interest to their remarks

Science and Technology Background

All moving objects have kinetic energy, the energy of motion. When a moving object collides with something that is not moving, kinetic energy is usually transferred from the moving object to the stationary one.

The amount of kinetic energy that a moving object has depends on two factors: the speed and the mass of the moving object. The kinetic energy

continueud

of a moving object is directly related to its mass—a 2-kg object will have twice the kinetic energy of a 1-kg object moving at the same speed. However, the kinetic energy of a moving object is also related to the square of its speed. So, if you triple the speed of an object, you have nine times the kinetic energy ($3^2 = 9$). This relationship is very important in collisions, especially in automobiles. For example, as an automobile moves from 30 km/h to 60 km/h, it has four times the kinetic energy.

If the stationary object can roll, like the marbles used in this activity, kinetic energy is transferred from the moving object to the stationary one. If the stationary object is fixed and cannot move, such as when an automobile runs into a tree, the kinetic energy is transferred into damage to the tree, the automobile, and its occupants.

When two objects collide, they still obey the law of conservation of energy (i.e., energy is not created nor destroyed in the collision). The moving object has kinetic energy, some of which will be transferred to the stationary object, while some can be transformed into other forms of energy such as sound energy, heat energy, and so on.

Get Started

Through an Activity

Roll a toy car into a stationary one on the front table or on the floor. Ask students, **What happened?** Responses should indicate that, in the beginning, one car was moving while the other was standing still. When the moving car hit the stationary one, the stationary one moved.

Through the Student Book

Have students read the Get Started paragraph individually. Ask, **What do you think when you hear the word "collision"? Have any of you ever run into an object on your bicycle? What happened?** Explain that today's lesson is going to look at what happens in a collision.

Work On It   PAIR

Ensure that the expectations for group work are clear. Marbles are objects that students often will begin to play with, so make sure that they know that this is a science experiment and that they should perform the investigation first. You may allow for free investigation with the marbles later on (see extension activity).

Remind students to read the procedure carefully, and to think about the data that they will need to collect. Advise them to create a data collection table before they begin.

Moving Marbles	Stationary Marbles	Observations
One (1)	Six (6)	
Two (2)	Five (5)	

Ask students, **What variables are we going to investigate in this activity?** (The number of stationary marbles and moving marbles will vary in each part.) If necessary, demonstrate how the materials are to be used in the investigation.

Have students carry out the investigation. Help pairs of students as necessary.

Assessing Students at Work

While students perform this activity, ask them about the ways they record the data and interpret it. What methods do they use? Why?

When students do steps 2, 3, and 4 in the procedure, it is important that they are aware of the need to keep the force with which they roll the marbles each time constant.

Communicate

Bring the class together. Check their understanding by asking: **What did you learn about collisions? What happens when a moving object hits one that is standing still?** (The moving object causes the stationary one to move. Some of the kinetic energy from the moving object is transferred to the stationary one.)

Question 1:

a. The kinetic energy from the one moving marble is transferred to the stationary marbles. The energy is transferred from marble to marble until it reaches the last one, which then uses that energy to start moving. One moving marble causes only one stationary marble to move.

b. The kinetic energy from the two moving marbles is transferred to the stationary marbles. The energy is transferred from marble to marble until it reaches the last two, which then uses that energy to start moving. Two moving marbles cause two stationary marbles to move.

c. The kinetic energy from the moving marble is transferred to the stationary marbles. The energy is transferred from marble to marble until it reaches the last one, which then uses that energy to start moving. One moving marble causes only one stationary marble to move more rapidly because the moving marble had more kinetic energy to start with.

d. The kinetic energy from the moving marble is transferred to the pencil and the pencil moves.

Question 2:

a. The hammer has kinetic energy that is transferred to the nail when it is hit. The kinetic energy in the nail causes it to go into the wood.

b. The ice-breaker has kinetic energy that is transferred to the ice-covered water. Some of the kinetic energy is transformed and will cause the ice to break, while other kinetic energy is transferred to the ice, causing it to move away, as the ice-breaker moves through the water.

Build On What You Know

Student pictures and descriptions will vary. In each, look for the student to explain how kinetic energy is transferred during the collision. For example, the kinetic energy in a kick is transferred to a stationary soccer ball and the ball moves away.

Extension

For Enrichment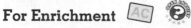

Have students use Activity Centre 6: Out of the Groove to do some free investigation using the marbles. They can come up with questions on their own, prepare a simple experiment, then test it. For example, students may wonder about collisions outside of the ruler groove, where one marble does not hit another directly in a straight line, similar to what happens on a pool or billiard table.

Have students research collisions. How does the automobile industry research collisions in order to make automobiles safer and more able to survive impacts with other objects? Students could research how air bags, bumpers, etc. work.

12 Motion and Environment

1–2 class periods

Skill Focus:
observing, inferring

Materials

No materials are required.

Learning Expectations

In this lesson students will:

> formulate questions about and identify needs and problems related to structures and mechanisms in the environment, and explore possible answers and solutions (LE 8)

> show an understanding of the impact of moving mechanisms on the environment and on living things (LE 18)

Lesson at a Glance

This lesson is a reading assignment that gives students information about the impact of machines and moving devices on the environment. It focuses on the beneficial effects of the Industrial Revolution in making our lives easier, as well as the social and environmental costs.

Curriculum Connections

In this lesson, students have the opportunity to develop skills and concepts in these areas:

Mathematics:
Measurement
• relate time, distance, and speed: kilometres per hour

Social Studies:
Developing Inquiry/Research and Communication Skills
• use appropriate vocabulary to describe their inquiries and observations
• formulate questions to serve as a guide to gathering information
• analyse, classify, and interpret information

Language Arts:
Writing
• use verb tenses consistently throughout a piece of writing
• frequently introduce vocabulary from other subject areas into their writing
Reading
• summarize and explain the main ideas in information materials and cite details that support the main ideas
• make judgments and draw conclusions about ideas in written materials on the basis of evidence
• select appropriate reading strategies
• plan a research project and carry out the research
• identify different forms of writing and describe their characteristics
• use their knowledge of the characteristics of different forms of writing to select the appropriate materials for a specific purpose
• use their knowledge of the elements of grammar and the structure of words and sentences to understand what they read
• consult a dictionary to confirm pronunciation and/or find the meaning of unfamiliar words
• understand specialized words or terms, as necessary
Oral and Visual Communication
• use a varied vocabulary and a range of sentence structures to add interest to their remarks

- speak correctly, observing common grammatical rules such as subject-verb agreement, noun-pronoun agreement, and consistency of verb tense

Science and Technology Background

Although humans have always had an effect on the environment, the Industrial Revolution began a new era in the way in which humanity shaped the natural world. The main feature of the Industrial Revolution was a dramatic increase in per capita production that was made possible by the mechanization of manufacturing and other processes that were carried out in factories. Its main social impact was that it changed an agrarian society into an urban industrial society.

The steam engine led to tractors that increased the amount of food a farmer could produce, a mechanized textile industry that clothed and employed more people, as well as steam locomotives, and eventually, the automobile that let people travel further and in shorter times. But the price of progress was costly. The shift from a rural agrarian society to an urban industrialized society led to crowded housing conditions, dirty water, increased diseases, and pollution-filled cities. We can see the effects of our machines on the environment everyday.

Although the historical term **Industrial Revolution** can be applied to specific countries and periods of the past, the process known as industrialization is still going on, particularly in developing countries, and the impact is just as severe.

Get Started

Through an Activity

Have students imagine they lived 300 years ago in a small farming village. The most complex machines were horse-drawn carts. Ask, **What is life like? What does the countryside around you look like?** Now have them imagine that they are transported to a city 100 years ago. There are factories and machines everywhere. Everyone they know works in a factory. Ask, **How would life be different? How would the environment be different?** Have students record their thoughts in a poem or journal entry.

Through the Student Book

Have students read the Get Started paragraph individually. Ask, **What machines do you use? How do they make your life easier?** Encourage students to name as many machines as possible. How do those machines affect the environment as they make your life easier? Students should be able to identify air and water pollution as consequences of the use of machines.

Work On It

Read the information on Student Book pages 32 and 33 as a class or individually. Ask students to suggest other examples of how machines affect the environment.

Ask, **Is the Industrial Revolution over?** Students may have read about the problems of increasing industrialization in developing countries around the world.

Assessing Students at Work

This is an opportunity to assess how well students can read for understanding. Assess students' understanding by having them summarize the meaning of the information in this section in their own words.

To help students understand the content of this lesson, tell them that they are going to be detectives looking for the answers to certain questions. Post questions for each paragraph on the board. Read each paragraph aloud, sentence by sentence, asking students to restate the sentence in their own words. After a paragraph has been read, ask students to answer the posted questions. Students must prove their answers by referring to specific parts of the text.

• Focus on Literacy •

Add new vocabulary to the ongoing class chart with your students:

Word	Picture or Symbol	Connected Words	Word in a Sentence
Social		society	
minimize		mini, minuscule	
agrarian		agriculture	
urban		urbs=city (Latin)	
disposal		dispose	
compounded		com=together	
consumers		consume	

Communicate

Bring the class together after the reading. Check their understanding by asking for examples of how machines affect the environment.

Question 1: Student answers will vary, but should suggest that machines made people able to accomplish more work and to make their lives easier.

Question 2: Student answers will vary. The Industrial Revolution changed European and North American society from agrarian to urban. People moved from farms to cities to look for work. Machines allowed industries to form and more products were available to all.

Question 3: Student answers will vary. Industries used machines to do the work that was formerly done by people alone. These machines and the urban-dwelling people that ran them led to crowded, unsanitary housing and air and water pollution.

Question 4: Student answers will vary. Our current lifestyle puts a heavy burden on the environment to supply the raw materials and to absorb the waste from the products we purchase every day.

Question 5: Student answers might include the automobile (pollution), public transit vehicles (less pollution), washing machine (waste water), sewing machine (making clothes means fewer products to buy), bicycle (environmentally friendly way to travel).

Question 6: Student answers will vary. Walking, bike, bus, and automobile go from least to most environmental impact. Distance you travel, speed and time you have, weather, etc. all affect a person's choice of how she or he gets to school.

Extension

For Enrichment

It has been said that we are currently living in the Information Revolution. Have students research how the computer has changed our lives and the way that work is done.

Assessment Follow-up

Students' responses to the Get Started and Communicate questions will allow you to assess their ability to identify needs and problems related to structures and mechanisms in the environment, and to explore possible solutions (LE 8), as well as their understanding of the impact of moving mechanisms on the environment and on living things (LE 18).

13 Handbook for Young Inventors

1–2 class periods

Skill Focus:
observing, inferring, interpreting, communicating

Materials

No materials are required.

Bookshelf

Caney, Steven, *Steven Caney's Invention Book* (Workman Publishing, 1985).

Taylor, Barbara, *Be An Inventor* (Harcourt Brace Jovanovich, 1987).

Learning Expectations

In this lesson students will:

> communicate the procedures and results of investigations for specific purposes and to specific audiences (LE 12)

> make use of the physical and aesthetic properties of natural and manufactured materials when designing a product (LE 13)

> show awareness of the effect on a design of the unavailability of specific materials (LE 14)

> write a plan outlining the different materials and processes involved in producing a product (LE 15)

> identify various criteria for selecting a product (LE 16)

> describe modifications that could improve the action of a variety of devices in the home (LE 17)

Lesson at a Glance

This lesson gives students a brief overview of how new products go from concept to finished product. Although there are no rules to how this happens, this reading assignment provides students with general information about the work that goes into new products, whether it's a new computer or the games that run on it.

Curriculum Connections

In this lesson, students have the opportunity to develop skills and concepts in these areas:

Social Studies:

Developing Inquiry/Research and Communication Skills
- use appropriate vocabulary to describe their inquiries and observations
- formulate questions to serve as a guide to gathering information
- communicate information, using media works, oral presentations, written notes and descriptions, drawings, tables, charts, maps, and graphs

Language Arts:

Writing
- use verb tenses consistently throughout a piece of writing
- integrate media materials into their writing to enhance their message

Reading
- summarize and explain the main ideas in information materials and cite details that support the main ideas
- make judgments and draw conclusions about ideas in written materials on the basis of evidence
- select appropriate reading strategies
- plan a research project and carry out the research
- use their knowledge of the characteristics of different forms of writing to select the appropriate materials for a specific purpose
- consult a dictionary to confirm pronunciation and/or find the meaning of unfamiliar words
- understand specialized words or terms, as necessary
- use punctuation to help them understand what they read
- use a variety of conventions of formal texts to find and verify information

Oral and Visual Communication
- use a varied vocabulary and a range of sentence structures to add interest to their remarks
- speak correctly, observing common grammatical rules such as subject-verb agreement, noun-pronoun agreement, and consistency of verb tense

Science and Technology Background

New products come on the market everyday. But they don't just get there by chance. It's a lot of hard work and a procedure that is similar to what a scientist does to investigate a problem. In the same way there is a method that scientists use to produce an experiment, there is a method to what gets a new product onto the market. This method involves market research, design and prototyping, design refinements, manufacturing, and marketing.

Get Started

Through an Activity
Ask students if they can think of any machines they use today that didn't exist when they were younger. Students may also be able to suggest machines used today that didn't exist when their parents were children. Ask, **Have you ever wondered how these new machines came to exist?**

Through the Student Book
Ask students, **Have you ever started your own business, like dog walking, a lemonade stand, mowing lawns, or shovelling snow? What did you do?**

Have students read the Get Started paragraph individually. Ask, **How is what you did different than what a large company would do if it wanted to make a new product or service, like a skateboard, computer program, or restaurant?** Students may think that the large company just does it on a bigger scale. Explain that businesses are organized and use procedures, similar to the scientific method, to ensure that their ideas for a product or service will make it to market. In this reading, students will learn about steps that new products go through before they get to market.

Work On It PAIR

Ask students, **Have you ever had someone ask you questions about what you liked or didn't like?** This could have been part of an opinion survey or market research, when someone talks to you or your parents on the telephone or had you or your parents fill out a questionnaire at a shopping mall. Explain that this is often the first step in starting a new company or making a new product. There are several other steps involved that they will read about in this section.

Have students work in pairs to read the information on Student Book pages 34 and 35. When pairing students to read the material, pair a stronger with a weaker reader. Tell students what you want them to find out through their reading by giving them questions for each paragraph. Have the stronger reader then read a paragraph out loud while the weaker one follows. The stronger reader reads the paragraph again while the weaker stops him when he comes to a part that gives the answer to a posted question.

Assessing Students at Work

This is an opportunity to assess how well students can read for understanding. Assess students' understanding by having them summarize the meaning of the information in this section in their own words.

13

Review the students' lists of the steps necessary to develop a product in order to assess their ability to write a plan outlining the different materials and processes involved in producing a product (LE 15) and to identify various criteria for selecting a product (LE 16).

Question 3 in Communicate allows you to assess students' ability to make use of the physical and aesthetic properties of natural and manufactured materials when designing a product (LE 13), and their awareness of the effect on a design of the unavailability of specific materials (LE 14).

Communicate

Bring the class together after they have read the assignment. Ask students, **Can you give me an example of a new product or service that has come on the market in the last year?** Students may identify a new computer game, a new television show, new action figures, etc.

Select one product they name and ask, **What steps could the company have done before the product was sold to the public?** Students may identify many of the steps they read about—market testing, prototyping, patent, and manufacturing processes.

Question 1:
a. Student answers will vary. Focus group questions could include: *Do you currently use in-line skates? What are the problems with current in-line rollerblades when you use them over rough terrain? Would you use/like/buy a new pair of in-line rollerblades if they could be used over rough terrain?*
b. Student answers could include other students, parents, athletes, etc.

Question 2: Student answers will vary. Students might say that new products can be designed on computers, tests on the product can be simulated on the computer and the design can be sent to other computers that control manufacturing.

Question 3:
a. Student answers will vary. Steel scissors are more durable, but plastic costs less. Some scissors use both, with steel edges on the blade and plastic handles.
b. Student answers will vary. Plastic is lighter and costs less to manufacture, but aluminum has a better look and more solid feel. Since it is an electrical device, the design might be different because plastic is an insulating material while aluminum conducts electricity and heat.
c. Student answers will vary. Steel would be more durable and able to withstand the shocks of the mountain trail. Plastic would be lightweight and cheaper, but would be difficult to make strong enough for the mountain trails.

Question 4: Student answers will vary. For example, students could take a product and change the kind of materials that are used in it so that recycled materials are used (e.g., use recycled plastic or metal).

Extension

For Enrichment

Have students research new products. What are the new products going to be for the next year? Often new products are highlighted in consumer or science magazines. Compare the predictions of previous years. How many were accurate?

Have students investigate the effects of fads on student spending. How does a new product become a fad? How long do fads last?

End-of-Unit Assessment Opportunities

Addison Wesley Science and Technology provides a range of opportunities for end-of-unit assessment and evaluation:

The **Design Project** enables you to assess how your students work to design a solution to a real-world problem. Students work in groups over 2–3 class periods. Students can be encouraged to record the process they followed to design their solution on Line Master 3: Design Project Planner. Line Master 4: Design Project Rubric will help you evaluate students' achievement with their design projects.

Demonstrate What You Know provides a paper-and-pencil individual performance assessment task that can be used to evaluate how well students perform after they have worked through the unit. Each Demonstrate What You Know is designed to touch on four areas of evaluation: students' ability to understand basic concepts, to demonstrate skills of inquiry and design, to relate their science learning to the world outside school, and to communicate their understanding. This task might also be used as a unit review, as an alternative to the design project, or as another task for students whose work on the design project was unsatisfactory.

Line Master 6: Student Self-Assessment Rubric can be used by students to assess their work in this individual assessment task. You might also share this rubric with students before they begin so they are aware of how they will be assessed and evaluated on this task.

Explain Your Stuff provides short answer questions to test students' basic knowledge of the concepts in the unit. Line Master 7: Explain Your Stuff can be used for students to record their answers. Questions could be assigned near the end of class. Those students who do not finish can take it home for homework. You may wish to collect and mark the questions, assigning half the mark for basic concepts and the other half relating science and technology to the world outside school. Record students' marks on copies of Line Master 2: End-of-Unit Assessment Summary Chart.

An alternative test that is not reproduced in the Student Book can be found on Line Master 8: Unit Test.

How Did You Do? provides a chance for students to evaluate their progress. The questions that appear on this page are reproduced on Line Master 9: How Did You Do? Once complete, this Line Master can be attached to a report card to communicate with parents.

To gather the information available to you about individual students based on all these forms of summative assessment, use Line Master 2: End-of-Unit Assessment Summary Chart. A filled-in sample of this chart is provided. You can record your assessment of students in any way that you feel comfortable.

The first two columns can be used to record an achievement level (1–4) for each of the four areas of the curriculum based on students' achievement with the Design Project and Demonstrate What You Know task. In the third column, a mark may be entered based on students' achievement with the Explain Your Stuff questions or Unit Test. This mark can then be converted to an achievement level (1–4). The last column can be filled in with a check mark or anecdotal comment to note that the students' self-reflection was considered complete. If the reflection was considered incomplete or unacceptable, it may be returned with teacher comments and students given another opportunity to complete the reflection questions. Depending on your science program, you may not wish to fill out all columns.

The information from Line Master 2, in conjunction with evidence gathered throughout the unit, can help you to determine the students' level of achievement for this unit.

Motion				Line Master 2

End-of-Unit Assessment Summary Chart

Student's name: _Rani_

	Design Project	Demonstrate What You Know	Explain Your Stuff	How Did You Do?
Understanding Basic Concepts	3	2		
Inquiry and Design Skills	2	3	$\frac{11}{16}$	Self-reflection questions showed little thought. Rani to work on them further.
Communication of Required Knowledge	2	2		
Relating of science and technology to each other and to the world outside the school	3	2		

© Addison Wesley Longman Ltd.   Motion **59**

Line Master 2: End-of-Unit Assessment Summary Chart

Science & Technology	B			Rani shows some understanding of motion and the way simple machines work. She recognizes how some machines are used in the world around her. She needs to become more aware of safety issues. Rani's written answers are appropriate but often incomplete.

Sample Report Card Comment

Design Project: Design Your Own Machine!

2–3 class periods

Skill Focus:
*predicting,
comparing,
communicating,
inferring*

Materials for each group

- paper
- pencil
- pencil crayons or felt pens
- various materials for prototype

Optional Materials

- the game *Mousetrap*

Learning Expectations

In this lesson students will:

> design and make mechanical devices that change the directions and speed of an input to produce a desired output and that perform a useful function (LE 7)

> formulate questions about and identify needs and problems related to structures and mechanisms in the environment, and explore possible answers and solutions (LE 8)

> plan investigations for some of these answers and solutions, identifying variables that need to be held constant to ensure a fair test and identify criteria for assessing solutions (LE 9)

> write a plan outlining the different materials and processes involved in producing a product (LE 15)

> identify various criteria for selecting a product (LE 16)

Lesson at a Glance

This lesson lets students represent their learning for this unit through the design and building of a model of a new, fantastic device—a model of a Rube Goldberg-type invention that shows several types of motion. Students are encouraged to use all the skills and knowledge they have gained while working on this unit.

Science and Technology Background

Rube Goldberg was an American cartoonist who produced many drawings of machines that use a complicated and often humorous series of steps to achieve a simple task. Many of the devices that he drew involved various types of motion.

Get Started

Through the Student Book

Have students read the Get Started paragraph individually.

If possible, set up the game *Mousetrap*. Trip the device and have students watch it work. Ask, **What types of motion do you see?**

Advise students that this project will give them an opportunity to design, build, and explain their own device similar to the game *Mousetrap*. This game uses an idea similar to what cartoonist Rube Goldberg drew.

Work On It

As students are forming their groups to work on this project, ensure that there is individual accountability, and that all group members participate equally and get a chance to represent their learning in the finished product.

Remind students to read all the steps in the Work On It introduction and Procedure so they have a better idea of what they are going to do in the investigation. Students should also read the questions in Communicate so they'll know what they are going to be asked after the activity is over.

It is sometimes difficult for students to think of a device to make. To stimulate ideas, tell students: **Sometimes the best ideas for an invention come from thinking about tasks that you already do. What kind of device could you build that would make your life easier?** Another way to spark ideas is to have students decide on a project that they are capable of building. Each student group should be directed toward a project that is at their appropriate level of development. Simple mechanical devices that use various kinds of motion work

Have students brainstorm their ideas as outlined in Procedure step 1.

You can either have students bring materials from home to build the projects, or limit them to a supply that you provide. As students carry out their project, assist groups as necessary.

Communicate

Bring the class together after they have completed the assignment. Check their understanding by asking questions during the process about the devices they built and the motion involved in it.

Question 1: Student answers will vary.
a. Students should identify the simple machines in their device.

b. Students should identify the kinds of motion in their device.

c. Students should list the science ideas that are demonstrated in their device, including linked motion.

Question 2: Student answers will vary. Students should explain how forces and kinetic energy are involved in the device.

Question 3: Student answers will vary. The point system is listed on Student Book page 37.

Question 4: Students will demonstrate their machine to the class.

Build On What You Know
Students will look for pictures of Rube Goldberg devices and will write a brief description telling of the motion the device has.

Extension

For Enrichment
Have students research Rube Goldberg to supplement the Build On What You Know section. Who was he? When did he do his work? Was he liked by his readers? How does he compare to current cartoonists?

Unit Review

Demonstrate What You Know

This assessment task provides students with an opportunity to demonstrate their understanding of several of the key concepts presented in the unit. It allows each student an opportunity to share what they know and have learned through the unit.

Students should be encouraged to use their notes and any relevant observations they have made. Assessment tasks like this one challenge students to apply their understanding and any new information they have acquired in new contexts and, through this experience, develop a deeper understanding of the material.

Overview

The unit review questions provide an opportunity for students to apply much of what they have learned in this unit to a single design problem. Concepts include simple machines, linked motion, effort, as well as general science concepts such as planning investigations and communicating results.

Application

This task could address a number of situations. Some possibilities are:
- Students who are absent during the Design Project may require an assessment task to demonstrate what they know. These students should be encouraged to use the information in the Design Project to help them with this task.
- Students may require another assessment task if they have completed the Design Project in a manner that is deemed unsatisfactory.
- Students may use Demonstrate What You Know to help them review the unit.

Evaluating Student Work

(1) The student should include both a sketch and a description of the mechanical system that will clean the chalkboards. They should include levers, linkages, and various kinds of motion to make their system. The chalkboard could be cleaned using linear, rotational, reciprocating, or osciallating motion. Students may include information about the forces that cause the motion and ways to reduce friction. If levers are used, students should identify the class the lever is and how it operates. Finally, students should include information about linkages and how they are used in the system.

Two samples of students' completed work are provided to illustrate what you might expect from your students. They should not be considered exemplars. The first is a sample of a Level 4 answer, and the second a Level 3 answer, determined using the rubric in the Student Book. You should expect a range of answers; these are only to illustrate the kind of work you can expect.

The rubric presented under Communicate may be used by students for self-assessment. By filling in Line Master 3, students should be able to assess how well they completed the task in four categories. If students need to understand the rubric, they can use the checklist provided in Step 4 of Work On It. This checklist aligns with the four statements in the rubric and provides criteria for students to use. Students should know that each of the criteria will be assessed in the rubric.

Once self-assessments have been completed, use them to begin a discussion on how well the student did this task. One strategy to use is to identify which of the statements both of you agree is a fair assessment of the work. Then focus on areas where you feel the student's assessment does not reflect your assessment. Encourage students to support their decisions, then provide your evidence for your decision. Once both of you have a clear understanding of each other's views, reassess the work.

① Serafina could use a mechanical system like the one I drew to clean the chalkboards.

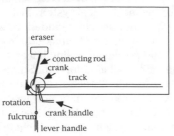

In my mechanical system, Serafina just has to turn the crank handle. This is rotational motion. This rotational motion turns the crank in a circle. The rotating crank is connected to the eraser by a connecting rod. The connecting rod moves up and down in reciprocating motion, which causes the eraser to move up and down as well. This up and down motion of the eraser cleans a vertical place on the chalkboard. But the rest of the chalk board also needs to be cleaned. The axle of the crank can also travels along a track in a linear motion. The crank is forced along the track by pulling the lever handle to the left. This is a first class lever. As the crank axle travels along the track, the eraser moves up and down from one side of the chalkboard to the other, cleaning the entire board.

Level 4 achievement

① Serafina could use a mechanical system like the one I drew to clean the chalkboards.

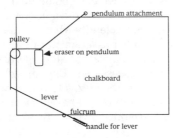

To operate the chalkboard cleaner, you push the lever handle up. This is a first class lever. The effort force is on the handle and the load force is on the rope that goes to the pendulum. This movement is linked to the rope that connects the lever to the pendulum and pulls down on the rope. The linear motion of the rope changes direction around the pulley and pulls the eraser on the pendulum toward the edge of the chalkboard. When you let go of the lever, the pendulum swings in oscillating motion back and forth across the chalkboard and cleans it.

Level 3 achievement

Explain Your Stuff

The questions on this page could be used as part of an end-of-unit test or an in-class review of the unit, among other possibilities. Provide students with a copy of Line Master 7 to record their answers. Examples of the types of answers you may expect are presented below:

Question 1: Student answers will vary. Sketches and descriptions could include:
a. linear motion—bicycle moving down the sidewalk
b. rotational motion—the wheels on the bicycle moving in a circle
c. reciprocating motion—the pistons in a car
d. oscillating motion—a swing

Question 2:
a. third class lever
b. second class lever
c. first class lever

Question 3: Student answers will vary. Friction is useful in a bicycle's brakes and with our feet pushing against the ground. Friction is not wanted in wheel bearings and wind pushing against the car.

Question 4: Student answers will vary. Students could suggest using wheels rather than pushing the box, or could make the surface of a ramp smoother and push the box up the ramp.

Question 5: Mohammed should move closer to the centre of the seesaw than Sarah.

Question 6: Kinetic energy is the energy of motion. All moving objects have kinetic energy.

Question 7: Omar's bicycle has kinetic energy because it is moving. When it collides with Yuhua's stationary bicycle, it will transfer some of it's kinetic energy to the stationary one, causing it to move.

Question 8: Student answers will vary. Students could show a lever, and show how it can change the direction and strength of a force.

Question 9: Student answers will vary. Students should describe how machines have made our lives easier, but that they have also had an impact on the environment through the use of resources for the manufacture or different kinds of pollution.

Question 10: Student answers will vary. Students should include ideas like market research, prototyping, patents, and manufacturing.

Question 11: Student answers will vary. Students may be interested in a wide variety of questions. For example, they could be interested in collisions, measuring motion, etc.

A set of multiple choice and short-answer questions based on the same content is included on Line Master 8: Unit Test for those students who require further review or testing, or whose needs are better served by varying the style of questioning.

Answers to the Unit Test can be found on page 77.

How Did You Do?

Students can answer these self-evaluation questions on copies of Line Master 9. The filled-in sheets could be attached to a report card for sharing with parents. Self-evaluation allows students to communicate their learning and their feelings about it. Seeing how students view their learning can give you insight and information on which to base your programming decisions.

Now you know a lot about motion! Here are some of the things you've learned:

This list is a summary of the main ideas that were presented in this unit. Discuss the statements in the list with the students. Ask, **Do you agree with these statements?** Invite students to expand on the statements by providing examples or evidence. This list can also be used by the students to quickly check their answers to the Explain Your Stuff questions.

If particular students have difficulty understanding or explaining these statements, you may wish to refer them to the activities listed below:

- There are four different kinds of motion: linear motion, rotational motion, reciprocating motion, and oscillating motion. Each kind of motion is important in various mechanical systems.

    p. 4 Kinds of Motion

    p. 7 Balloon Rockets in Motion

    p. 12 Pendulums

    p. 15 Circles into Lines

- Motion can be seen in many objects. Several kinds of motion are often involved in one machine.

    p. 15 Circles into Lines

    p. 28 Combining Simple Machines

- All motion is caused by a force.

    p. 9 Forces and Motion

    p. 17 Friction Can Be a Drag!

- Friction is a force that opposes motion. It transforms some of the kinetic energy of the moving object into heat energy. There are several ways that friction can be reduced.

    p. 17 Friction Can Be a Drag!

- There are six simple machines: the ramp, pulley, wedge, screw, lever, and wheel-and-axle. Every simple machine performs at least one of these functions: transfers a force, changes the direction of a force, or changes the strength of a force.

    p. 21 Simple Machines

- There are three classes of levers. Each class uses a different arrangement of the lever arm, fulcrum, effort force, and load force. Levers can be used either by themselves or linked to other levers and simple machines to transmit motion and force.

    p. 24 Levers

- All moving objects contain kinetic energy. When one object collides with another that is stationary, some of the kinetic energy is transferred from the moving object to the stationary one.

    p. 30 Collisions

- Machines that use motion have had an effect on society and the environment.

    p. 32 Motion and the Environment

Ongoing Assessment Tracking Sheet

Overall Expectations	Demonstrate an understanding of different kinds of motion (linear, rotational, reciprocating, oscillating)						Design and make mechanical devices, and investigate how mechanisms change one type of motion into another and transfer energy from one form into another						Identify modifications to improve the design and method of production of systems that have mechanisms that move in different ways							
Learning Expectations*	1	2	3	4	5	6	7	8	9	10	11	12	13	14	15	16	17	18	19	20
Student's Name																				

* See page 4 Curriculum Correlation for a list of the specific coded expectations

End-of-Unit Assessment Summary Chart

Student's name: _____

	Design Project	Demonstrate What You Know	Explain Your Stuff	How Did You Do?
Understanding Basic Concepts				
Inquiry and Design Skills				
Communication of Required Knowledge				
Relating of science and technology to each other and to the world outside the school				

Design Project Planner: Design Your Own Machine!

Group members: _____

Design for Your Machine

1 The problem that needs to be solved is:

_____

_____

2 This problem can be solved by:

_____

_____

The materials needed are:

_____

_____

Draw your design. (Use the back of the sheet if you need more space.)

3 Build your model from your design.

4 Test your design.
Do you need to make any changes to your design? Draw your revised design here.
(Use the back of the sheet if you need more space.)

5 This is a better design because:

_____

_____

Design Project Rubric

Student name(s): _____

Areas of Assessment	1	2	3	4
Basic Concepts • Shows understanding of the basic concept that linked actions are necessary for the machine to complete the task	The machine is unable to perform any linked actions ☐	The machine performs two linked actions with some assistance as it completes its task ☐	The machine performs at least three linked actions with minimal assistance as it completes its task ☐	The machine successfully performs three or more linked actions as it completes its task ☐
Skills • Designs, builds and tests a model of a Rube Goldberg-type machine to complete a specific task	Design, building, and test of model uses very few of the required skills and strategies ☐	Design, building, and test of model uses some of the required skills and strategies ☐	Design, building, and test of model demonstrates most of the required skills and strategies ☐	Design, building, and test of model demonstrates exceptional use of the required skills and strategies ☐
Communication • Describes and explains the applications of learned science principles within their machines	Descriptions and explanations are vague and unclear and do not include appropriate terminology ☐	Descriptions and explanations are somewhat clear and precise with minimal terminology used appropriately ☐	Descriptions and explanations are mostly clear and precise and include appropriate terminology ☐	Descriptions and explanations are very clear and precise and include all appropriate terminology ☐
Relating of Science & Technology to each other and to the world outside the school • After building and testing the model, students are able to identify and explain the science principles they have learned in this unit that are demonstrated by their machines	Shows little or no understanding of connections between science principles and the actions of the machine ☐	Shows some understanding of connections between science principles and the actions of the machine ☐	Shows a good understanding of connections between science principles and the actions of the machine ☐	Shows a complete understanding of connections between science principles and the actions of the machine ☐

Strand: Structures and Mechanisms

Student Achievement Summary

| Student's name | Levels of achievement from Design Project | | | | Highest most consistent level | Test(s) | Final Grade or Percent |
	Basic Concepts	Skills	Communi-cation	Science and Technology			

Student Self-Assessment Rubric

Name: _____

Demonstrate What You Know

How well do you think you did? Circle the phrase that you think applies to your work.

1 star	2 stars	3 stars	4 stars
★	★ ★	★ ★ ★	★ ★ ★ ★

- How much do you know about motion? Look at your labelled sketch and your description. Does your work show you know

A little about motion	Some information about motion	A lot of information about motion	All about motion?

- Look at the description of your design. Does your work show you have applied

A few of the skills to use levers and linkages to transfer force	Some of the skills to use levers and linkages to transfer force	Most of the skills to use levers and linkages to transfer force	All of the skills to use levers and linkages to transfer force?

- Now look again at your description. Will it be clear and precise to a reader?

Not very clear or precise	Somewhat clear and precise	Mostly clear and precise	Very clear and precise

- How well do you think you understand what Serafina wanted her mechanical system to do?

Not much understanding	Some understanding	A good understanding	A complete understanding

Here is how I would do better next time:

_____

_____

_____

Explain Your Stuff

Name: _____

1 Use a sketch to help describe an example of each kind of motion:

a. linear motion   b. rotational motion

c. reciprocating motion   d. oscillating motion

2 Identify the class of lever for each of the following devices.

a. staple remover

_____

b. nutcracker

_____

c. scissors

_____

3 Describe two situations where friction is useful. Give two examples where friction is not wanted.

_____

_____

_____

4 Jialing and Kendra have to move a heavy box to the top of a ramp. Describe two ways that friction could be reduced to move the box more easily.

_____

_____

_____

5 Mohammed and Sarah are on a seesaw. Mohammed is heavier than Sarah. How should Mohammed move in order for the two of them to be balanced?

_____

_____

6 What is kinetic energy? How is it related to motion?

_____

_____

7 Describe what happens when Omar's moving bicycle collides with Yuhua's stationary bicycle.

_____

_____

8 Use a sketch to help explain how a mechanical device can change the direction and strength of a force.

9 Explain how the use of mechanical devices has changed society. What impact did it have on the environment?

_____

_____

10 Describe the steps you might take if you had an idea for a new product and wanted to produce it for sale.

_____

_____

11 If you could investigate one question about motion, what would it be? How would you go about doing this investigation?

_____

_____

Unit Test

Name: _____

1. Match the kind of motion with each example
   a. pistons in a car   linear motion
   b. hockey puck sliding on ice   rotational motion
   c. playground swing   reciprocal motion
   d. Ferris wheel at an amusement park   oscillating motion

2. Draw a picture of a first, second, or third class lever. Label which type of lever you have drawn. Show and label the lever arm, fulcrum, and location of the effort force and load.

3. You have to move a heavy box from the floor to the stage. Explain how you could perform the task as easily as possible.

   _____

   _____

4. Explain what happens when Jason's moving bicycle collides with a stationary garbage can in front of Jason's home.

   _____

   _____

5. If you wanted a pendulum to swing faster, which of the following would you do:
   a. give it a lighter weight on the end of the string
   b. decrease the arc it swings
   c. shorten the string
   d. all of the above

6 There are six simple machines. Choose one and explain how it works and performs its function.

_____

_____

_____

7 Which of the following statements are true:
a. All moving objects move in a straight line.
b. All moving objects have kinetic energy.
c. All moving objects involve a mechanical device.

8 True or False: All friction is bad. Explain your answer.

_____

_____

_____

9 A factor that affects the outcome of an experiment is called a

_____.

10 Explain the effects machines have on our lives. List two good things and two bad things.

_____

_____

_____

_____

_____

_____

_____

_____

_____

How Did You Do?

Name: _____

1 List three surprising or unexpected things that you discovered in the unit on motion.

_____

_____

_____

_____

_____

2 What was your favourite activity in this unit? Why? Which was your least favourite activity?

_____

_____

_____

_____

_____

3 Give yourself three compliments about the way you participated in this unit on motion. What did you do well?

_____

_____

_____

_____

_____

_____

4 List three questions that you would like to answer the next time you study motion.

_____

_____

_____

_____

_____

The Inquiry Process for Science

Name: _____

❶ My question is...

_____

_____

❷ My plan for my investigation is...

_____

_____

_____

_____

_____

_____

_____

❸ Here are my observations and data I collected.

_____

_____

_____

_____

_____

_____

❹ My conclusion is...

_____

_____

❺ I will share my findings by...

_____

_____

The Design Process for Technology

Name: _____

❶ The problem that needs to be solved is...

_____

_____

❷ Here is the plan for my design, with a labelled drawing and a list of materials.

❸ Now I'll build my design.

❹ I will test my design. Do I need to make any changes to my design? Here is my revised design.

❺ I will share my design by...

_____

_____

Design Challenge:
The Ultimate Balloon Rocket!

The Problem

You have experimented with making horizontal rockets. Now your task is to design and build a rocket that will go the farthest along an 8-m long piece of string.

Plan Your Design

Think about the horizontal balloon rockets you have built. What changes in the design of your balloon rocket will make it travel farther?

List your ideas. Pick one idea that you would like to try. What materials will you need to build it?

Draw a picture of what your set-up will look like. Remember to make your plan clear enough that someone else could follow it.

Build Your Design

Build your balloon rocket. Does it look and work like you want it to?

Test Your Design

Is there anything else that could be added to the rocket that might make it go farther? Test your ideas until you find the best combinations.

Communicate

Which of your designs allowed your rocket to travel the furthest along the string? Write a short paragraph describing what you found out. Which design was the best one? Why?

All Fall Down!

Does the size of a parachute determine the speed that an object falls through the air?

Materials
two equal-sized balls of clay
ruler
15 cm x 15 cm piece of plastic
  cut from a garbage bag
scissors

string
tape
30 cm x 30 cm piece of plastic
  cut from a garbage bag

Procedure

1. Look at the pieces of plastic cut from the garbage bag. Predict which one will slow the fall of the ball of clay through the air the best.

2. Attach 20-cm pieces of string to the four corners of the smaller piece of plastic.

3. Bring the other ends of the string together and tie in a knot.

4. Use the tape to attach the string to one ball of clay.

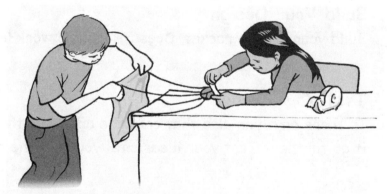

5. Repeat the process with the larger piece of plastic.

6. Drop each parachute from the same height, such as above your head or the top of the playground slide.

What Did You Find Out?
Which of the parachutes slowed the fall of the ball of clay the most? How could you tell? Draw a diagram indicating the forces acting in each case. Was your prediction correct?

Design Challenge: Make Time

The Problem
Now you have learned a lot about pendulums. Your task is to design and build a pendulum that will accurately measure one minute.

Plan Your Design
With a partner, think about the pendulums you have built. What changes in the design of your pendulum will allow it to accurately measure one minute?

Draw a picture of what your pendulum will look like. Include specific measurements and details about the length of the string, the mass, and the arc length of the pendulum swing that you will use. Remember to make your plan clear enough that someone else could follow it.

Build Your Design
Build your pendulum. Does it look and work like you want it to?

Test Your Design
Start the stopwatch at the same time as you start swinging your pendulum.

When the pendulum has finished swinging, stop the watch. How close were you to one minute? If necessary, redesign your pendulum. Remember to change only one variable at a time and to record any changes on your plan.

Continue to redesign and test your pendulum until it comes as close as possible to measuring one minute.

Communicate
Were you able to build a pendulum that accurately measures one minute? Did you have to revise your initial design? Demonstrate your pendulum for your classmates.

Return of the Balloon Rocket

Do you remember the balloon rocket you made in Activity 2: Balloon Rockets in Motion? Does the kind of string the balloon rocket travels down make a difference to how far it travels?

Materials

oblong balloons	8 m string
8 m nylon line (fishing line)	drinking straw
chair	desk
tape	ruler or measuring tape
pencil	scissors

Procedure

1. Look at the string and nylon line. If an identical balloon rocket travels along each one, predict which will allow the balloon rocket to travel the farthest. Explain your thinking.

2. Thread the string through the straw. Tie one end of the string to the leg of a desk. Tie the other end to a chair. Move the chair away from the desk so that the string is taut and as level as possible. Repeat the process with the nylon line.

3. Blow up a balloon. Twist the end closed. Note the size of the balloon now that it is filled with air. One member of your group will hold it closed until step 4.

4. Tape the balloon to the straw on the string. Slide the straw along the string until the twisted end of the balloon is next to the desk.

5. Carefully release the twisted end of the balloon. Measure the distance your balloon rocket travelled.

6. Repeat steps 2 to 4, only this time tape the balloon to the straw on the nylon line. Remember that the balloon should be the same size when filled with air as the balloon in the first part of the experiment.

What Did You Find Out?

Was your prediction correct? Which balloon travelled the farthest? Explain why you think this happened. What role did friction play in the results of the experiment?

Design Challenge: The Tree House

The Problem

You and a group of friends have decided to build a tree house. You collect the wood, nails, tools, and other materials you need to build it. However, you have one problem. How can you get the materials up into the tree as needed with as little effort as possible? Your task is to design a simple machine to help you move the materials.

Plan Your Design

With a partner, think of different simple machines that you could build to move the materials. Keep a list of your ideas. Remember, there are no right or wrong answers, just ideas.

Review your list. Is there one idea you think will work best? The idea should be something that you and a group of friends could accomplish. What materials will you need to build the machine?

Draw a picture of your plan for the machine. Label all the parts and describe how your machine will perform the task. Make sure your plan is clear enough so that someone else could follow it and build the machine. Have your teacher check your work before you go on.

Build Your Design

Build a model of your machine.
Does it look and work like you want it to?

Test Your Design

If you now want to make any changes to your design, don't forget to note the changes on your plan.

Communicate

After you've completed your task, write a short paragraph about what you learned during this activity. Include any information that might help other students who do this activity.

Out of the Groove

Think about how you tested marble collisions. What do you think happen if the marbles collided outside of the ruler groove? Consider the following questions:

1. What will happen when a moving marble collides with another identical marble that is stationary and it hits straight on?
2. What will happen when a moving marble collides with another identical marble that is stationary and it hits at an angle?
3. What will happen when a marble moves at different speeds and collides with another identical marble that is stationary?

Materials
2 identical marbles
large, open, flat space

Procedure

❶ Choose one of the above questions to investigate.

❷ Make a prediction about what you think will happen in the investigation you have chosen.

❸ Design an investigation that will let you test your prediction. Remember that in any investigation, only one variable can be changed while the other variables stay the same. How will you make sure your test is fair?

❹ Record your observations so that you can describe what happened during your investigation.

What Did You Find Out?
Write a short paragraph about what you found out in your investigation. Use diagrams to help with your description.

Unit Test Answers

1. a) pistons in a car—reciprocal motion
    b) hockey puck sliding on ice—linear motion
    c) playground swing—oscillating motion
    d) Ferris wheel at amusement park—rotational motion

2. First class lever   second class lever   third class lever

    Lever arm —————   Fulcrum   △

    Load   •   Effort force   ↓

3. Make an inclined plane (ramp) from the floor to the stage (using a board), then slide the box up the ramp.

4. The kinetic energy from the motion of Jason's bicycle is transferred to the garbage can causing the garbage can to move and/or dent.

5. If you wanted a pendulum to swing faster, which of the following would you do:
    d) all of the above

6. inclined plane (ramp)—changes the direction and strength of a force (i.e., a horizontal effort force moves the object horizontally and vertically)

    pulley—changes the direction or strength of a force (a fixed pulley changes direction of a force, a movable pulley reduces the effort force)

    wedge—changes the direction of a force (produces force at right angles to the effort force) (the strength of the lateral force depends on the angle of the wedge)

    screw—changes a rotational force into a linear force and reduces the effort force

    lever—changes the direction and/or strength of a force

    wheel and axle—changes a linear force into a rotational force and reduces the effort force (and reduces friction)

7. Which of the following statements are true:
    b) all moving objects have kinetic energy

8. All friction is bad. **False**. Friction enables us to stop cars (brakes), move (friction between feet and ground or tires and road), and fly kites or parachute (air resistance).

9. A factor that affects the outcome of an experiment is called a **variable**.

10. A number of answers would be acceptable (e.g., machines allow us to move quickly from place to place, lift heavy objects, split wood etc., but machines can also hurt or kill us, pollute the environment, cause loss of natural habitats, use up resources, and so on.

Teaching Notes

Teaching Notes

Teaching Notes